SMALL SCALE INDUSTRY

SMALL SCALE INDUSTRY

SUCCESS AND FAILURE

VINOD K TEWARI
JOSEPH PHILIP
AMAR NATH PANDEY

CONCEPT PUBLISHING COMPANY, NEW DELHI 110059

ISBN 81-7022-364-4

First Published 1991

Published and Printed by
Concept Publishing Company
A/15-16, Commercial Block, Mohan Garden
NEW DELHI 110059 (India)

Lasertypeset by
Microtech Advance Printing Systems (Pvt.) Ltd.
H-13, Bali Nagar
NEW DELHI 110015

PREFACE

It is interesting to discover as to what motivates individuals to set up a small scale unit inspite of known obstacles in achieving success in this sector. The most important motivating factor the study reveals is non-economic. It is the desire to be self-employed — to prove one's capability and to gain social prestige. Apparently the desire to make economic gains is only secondary. However, an overwhelming majority of the entrepreneurs had previous work experience which suggests that the ambition to be self-employed is not entirely blind. It appears to acquire legs only after a measure of experience and self-confidence has been gained while working for others; though "dissatisfaction" with the previous job does act as a propellant.

While taking the jump the entrepreneurs seem to rely more on their own ability and skills relative to the availability of financial and material resources. But in the real world financial resources and market support are crucial for success. The inadequacy of these, the study shows, has acted as a major constraint — affecting progress or leading to failure. This implies the failure of public policy and programmes to neutralise constraints which are beyond the power of individual entrepreneurs — no matter how skilled, self-confident or motivated.

Another important characteristic of small entrepreneurs confirmed by the study is that mostly they want to make a beginning with a small quantum of capital with minimal debt. They contribute significantly (nearly one third) of the required resources from their own savings or that of their relatives or friends. In contrast the policy continues to be preoccupied with raising the investment limit higher and higher without arranging for adequate credit even at lower levels of investment.

An analysis of successful and sick units reveals that the unsuccessful entrepreneurs did not have any marked lack of motivation, skills and past experience compared with the successful entrepreneurs. A possible answer may be that failure was due largely to factors external to the firm. The needle of suspicion turns on macro policy which if it aims to support small scale entrepreneurs in selected products must ensure that the market space meant to be occupied by the output of small scale enterprises is not encroached upon by others. To what extent this has been a factor in the case of sample units which were sick has not been sufficiently investigated by this study — presumably leaving it for successor studies to explore.

Last but not the least, is the contribution of the small units to employment. The annual growth rate of employment for all the sample units was 7 per cent (range 2 to 13 per cent) which is double that expected of the manufacturing sector as a whole in the 8th Plan. This underscores the justification for continued policy support for the small scale on grounds of employment alone — and no less on grounds of creating avenues for self-employment which is the socially and psychologically preferred mode.

The literature on small scale is rare. A good study such as this is thus more than welcome.

23rd October, 1990

L.C. Jain
Member, Planning Commission

ACKNOWLEDGEMENTS

At the outset we wish to express our gratitude to the Karnataka State Financial Corporation (KSFC), Bangalore, for providing financial support for this important study in the field of small scale industries.

We are thankful to Shri M. Shankaranarayanan, IAS, Chairman, KSFC, who readily agreed to consider our request for financial support for the study at the initiation stage itself. Shri YK Puttasome Gowda, IAS, Managing Director, KSFC, took keen interest in the study and provided us the necessary guidance and support for which we are indeed grateful to him.

Our discussions with Dr YB Yalawar, General Manager, Shri SR Chandrashekar Shetty, General Manager, Shri K Shivappa, Asstt. General Manager, Shri RJ Fernandez, Asstt. General Manager, and Shri R Prabhakar and Shri S Prabhu both Dy Managers, all of KSFC, were very useful in shaping the study. We would like to thank all of them and acknowledge their contributions.

The Directorate of Industries and Commerce, Govt. of Karnataka, Karnataka State Small Scale Industrial Development Corporation, Small Industries Service Institutes, Hubli and Gulbarga, provided the necessary background information for the study. We would like to acknowledge the cooperation of Karnataka Small Scale Industries Association, Bangalore, Mysore Chamber of Commerce and Industry, Mysore, Peenya Industries Association, Bangalore, North Karnataka Small Scale Industries Association, Hubli, Mysore Industrial Estate Manufacturers' Association, Mysore, and Associations of SSI entrepreneurs at the ancillary industrial estates of HAL, HMT and ITI, all at Bangalore, in the course of field survey. The respondent-entrepreneurs are, in fact, informal partners in this research effort.

We would like to thank our colleague Prof P V George for his comments and suggestions on an earlier draft of the report. Our appreciation is due also to the project staff who helped us in the processing of data, and to Mr Mohd. Saifulla, who provided computer assistance in the production of the report.

Indian Institute of Management
Bangalore
March 12, 1990

VINOD K TEWARI
JOSEPH PHILIP
AMAR NATH PANDEY

CONTENTS

LIST OF TABLES

1

INTRODUCTION

Background

Small Scale Industries (SSI) have, of late, become a major force in furthering the process of rapid industrialisation in India. The total number of registered SSI units in India was 5.23 lakhs in the year 1981-82 and it had gone up to about 16 lakhs by the year 1987-88. The value of total production in the SSI sector had gone up from Rs. 32,600 crores to Rs. 85,000 crores, and the number of persons employed in the SSI sector had gone up from 75 lakhs to one crore during the same period. At the same time, the number of sick SSI units had gone up from 25,342 in the year 1981 to 1,58,226 in the year 1987. The outstanding bank credit against the sick SSI units had gone up from Rs. 395 crores in the year 1981 to Rs. 1542 crores in the year 1987. Thus, two somewhat contrastive trends — rapid growth and growing sickness had become prominent over the last few years.

It was felt that these two contrastive trends provided an opportunity for the identification and comparative analysis of factors causing and contributing to the success of SSI units on one hand, and those responsible for the failure of SSI units on the other. The outcome of such an exercise could provide useful guidelines for the review and restructuring of promotional policies and the schemes of financial and promotional support for the SSI sector. Also, it would be useful in preparing course-materials for training existing and potential entrepreneurs as well as those involved in extending financial and promotional support to SSI.

In this background, the present study on "Success and Failure of Small Scale Industrial Units" was undertaken by the authors.

Scope and Objectives

Such a study necessarily requires investigation and analysis of:

(i) age, form of organisation, nature of activity, product-type, size of investment, employment, turnover of a unit;
(ii) background profile of the entrepreneur comprising his age, education, training, work experience, income and parental background, etc.;
(iii) the factors that motivated him to set up a SSI unit, the factor that discouraged him, the problems that he faced in the process of setting up of his unit;
(iv) mobilisation of financial and other resources, operational problems of a unit, and the entrepreneur's efforts to overcome the problems; and
(v) a historical account of major developments in the unit, past and present performance of the unit, and future plan for the growth of unit.

Accordingly, the study was designed to achieve the following major objectives:

1. To examine –

- background of entrepreneurs;
- factors that motivated them to set up SSI units;
- factors considered for the selection of product;
- financial and other support received by entrepreneurs in setting up of their units;
- problems faced in the process of setting up of the units;
- operational problems faced in running the units;
- entrepreneurs' efforts to overcome the operational problems and others;
- performance of the units since their inception; and
- future plans for the growth of the units.

2. To make a comparative analysis of all the factors mentioned above (1) across the different performance-groups of SSI units.
3. To identify factors responsible for the varying group-performance.

4. To suggest necessary measures based on the findigs of the study.

Study Design

Questionnaire

For the purpose of the study, a questionnaire was designed for seeking necessary information from the sample entrepreneurs with regard to:

(i) the year of establishment, acquisition of unit, form of organisation;
(ii) nature of activity and product-type;
(iii) initial investment and cumulative investment till 1987-88 in fixed assets (plant and machinery);
(iv) number of persons employed, installed capacity and annual turnover;
(v) present status of unit;
(vi) age, education, training and experience of entrepreneur;
(vii) entrepreneur's income before the setting up of unit;
(viii) education and occupation of entrepreneurs' father/guardian;
(ix) motivating factors (ambition, compulsion, encouragement, expection and consideration);
(x) discouragement and problems in setting up of unit;
(xi) mobilization of financial resources by source, operational expenses, and problems faced;
(xii) efforts made to overcome the major problems, and turning points in the life of unit;
(xiii) factors responsible for the present level of performance;
(xiv) future plan for the growth of unit; and
(xv) willingness of entrepreneur to allow his unit to graduate to the medium scale level.

Another questionnaire was designed to seek additional information from sick SSI units with regard to:

(i) symptoms of sickness;
(ii) preventive measures;
(iii) declaration of sickness;
(iv) viability study of unit; and

(v) recommendation and implementations of rehabilitation measures, etc.

Study Area

Considering the location of the study group, possibility of getting financial support for the study from the Karnataka State Financial Corporation (KSFC), and rapid growth of SSI in Karnataka since 1969-70, it was decided that the study area would be confined to the State of Karnataka. Further, within the State, the field survey should be confined to the select sample districts and the sample districts should be representive of highly industrialised districts, moderately industrialised districts, and industrially backward districts of the State. After the financial support from KSFC for the present study was confirmed, four sample districts were selected in consultation with the concerned officials of KSFC. The four sample districts are (1) Bangalore—a highly industrialised district; (2) Mysore and Dharwar — moderately industrialised districts, and (3) Gulbarga — an industrially backward district. While Bangalore and Mysore districts are located in the southern part of Karnataka, Dharwar and Gulbarga districts are located in the northern part. A brief account of SSI in the study area is discussed in the last section of this chapter.

Selection of Sample Units

Within the constraint of limited financial resources available for the study it was decided, in consultation with KSFC, that the sample should consist of 120 SSI units spread over the four districts. Out of the total of 120 sample SSI units, 62 units were located in Bangalore District, 30 units in Mysore District, 16 units in Dharwar District, and 12 units in Gulbarga District. Before the selection of sample units, background information were obtained from KSFC, Directorate of Industries and Commerce, Government of Karnataka (GOK), Karnataka State Small Scale Industrial Development Corporation, Small Industries Service Institutes, and various associations of SSI entrepreneurs in Bangalore, Mysore and Dharwar. After a preliminary analysis of background information, a stratified purposive sampling design was evolved for the selection of sample SSI units. The sample units were selected on the basis of their age, product-type, and existing performance status.

Sample Survey

Prior to the commencement of the survey of sample SSI units, preliminary discussions were held with a group of SSI entrepreneurs at Bangalore and Mysore. In the course of discussion, it was realised that getting the required information from the sample entrepreneurs would not be an easy task, partly because of their busy schedules and partly because of lack of interest in the case of some of the sample entrepreneurs. It was, therefore, decided that:

- questionnairs should be sent in advance to the sample entrepreneurs through their respective associations;
- the date of interview with the individual entrepreneur should be fixed in advance; and
- principal investigators should conduct field investigation on their own rather than depending on research assistants.

As a result, all the 120 sample entrepreneurs were interviewed and the necessary information were obtained from them through a specially designed questionnaire by the principal investigators on their own. Even then, the field survey proved to be quite a formidable task mainly because of inadequate cooperation from some of the sample entrepreneurs. In many cases, multiple visits had to be made despite prior appointments and preliminary discussions with the concerned entrepreneurs. In a few cases, sample SSI units had to be substituted by similar units in the same district when repeated visits and reminders over phone failed to yield the result. The field survey commenced in the month of April 1988 and was completed towards the end of October, 1988.

A Brief Profile of Sample SSI Units

Out of 120 sample units:

- 81 per cent were more than five years old;
- 48 per cent of the units were proprietorship concerns;
- 39 per cent were partnership concerns;
- 12 per cent were private limited companies; and
- one unit was a co-operative society.

Sixty-three per cent of the units were engaged in manufacturing:

- 8 per cent in processing;
- 8 per cent in job-works; and
- 2 per cent in servicing.

The remaining units were engaged in a combination of activities.

- Forty-four per cent of the units were engineering units;
- 20 per cent electrical and electronic units;
- 12 per cent food and chemical units; and
- the remaining units were leather, rubber, plastic, paper, cement and wood units.

The size of investment in fixed assets (plant and machinery) in the year 1987-88 was:

- upto Rs. 2 lakhs or below in the case of 29 per cent of the units;
- between Rs. 2 lakhs and Rs. 5 lakhs in 30 per cent of the units;
- between Rs. 5 lakhs and Rs. 10 lakhs in 19 per cent of the units; and
- above Rs. 10 lakhs in remaining 22 per cent of the units.

Analysis and Organisation of Report

For the purpose of analysis, 98 sample SSI units (excluding 22 sick SSI units) were classified into three groups on the basis of:

- annual growth rate of investment on plant and machinery;
- annual growth rate of employment;
- annual growth rate of turnover;
- annual growth rate of investment on plant and machinery per employee;
- annual growth rate of total productive capital per employee;
- ratio of turnover to investment on plant and machinery;
- ratio of turnover to working capital; and
- ratio of turnover to total productive capital.

The growth rates of all the 98 units were ranked and based on the Average Composite Rank Index (ACRI) of each unit, these units were classified into:

- very successful group (VSU) comprising 18 units;
- successful group (SU) comprising 42 units; and
- average group (AVU) comprising 38 units.

The units with ACRI of less than 40 were classified as very successful units, those having ACRI between 40 and 60 as successful units and those having ACRI above 60 were classified as average units (Table 1.1).*

The 22 sick sample units were treated as a separate group. Thus, all the 120 sample SSI units were classified into four performance-groups.

The analysis of almost all the information collected from the sample units has been done as per the performance-groups as well as for the sample as whole. For the purpose of analysis, the statistical techniques, like cross tabulation, simple averages, weighted rank index, chi-square, compound rates of growth, and financial ratios, etc. have been used. A major limitation of the financial analysis is that it is based on historical prices and current prices. Since the year wise details of investment in different components of plant and machinery, and quantity of individual product items and sale value of each product

---

* The performance of 98 sample SSI units was estimated on the basis of economic criteria instead of mere profitability of a unit because:

1. Profitability of a unit is a very uncertain factor and unless profitability figures are available for a sufficiently long period of time or at least for a number of points of time, the success of a unit cannot be assessed realistically.
2. Break-ups of fixed costs and variable costs for a number of years are required for computing profitability of a unit and assessing its performance. However, inspite of the best efforts, the study team could not get the details of fixed costs and variable costs from most of the sample SSI units even for three years. This was because of (a) non-maintenance of such information by many of the sample entrepreneurs, (b) unwillingness of some of the sample entrepreneurs to provide these information, (c) difficulties in tracing back the old information, and (d) lack of time for furnishing such detailed information.
3. In such a situation it was decided to use only economic criteria, like growth rates of (a) capital investment, annual turnover and employment; (b) per employee investment and annual turnover indicating capital intensity and manpower utilization respectively; and (c) ratios of turnover to capital indicating efficiency levels of capital utilization. These criteria together can facilitate much sound assessment of performance of a unit than what mere profitability of a unit can.

item from the individual sample units (the same unit produced different items of varying dimensions and qualities) could not be obtained, it was not possible to work out the values of investment and turnover, etc. at constant prices.

TABLE 1.1: Average Composite Rank Index of Sample SSI Units belonging to the Different Performance Groups

Success Group/ Rank Index Range	Average Composite Rank Index*					
Very Successful Units (VSU) (< 40)	9.7	18.3	19.7	26.9	30.1	30.4
	31.0	32.3	33.4	34.3	34.4	34.6
	36.6	36.9	37.1	37.4	38.0	38.0
Successful Units (SU) (40 — 60)	40.3	40.6	41.0	41.1	41.9	42.0
	42.0	43.1	43.4	43.7	44.1	45.4
	45.7	46.4	46.9	47.1	47.1	47.8
	48.1	48.8	49.0	49.1	50.0	51.8
	52.4	52.5	53.6	54.0	54.2	54.3
	55.3	56.6	57.7	57.7	58.7	59.3
	59.8	60.0	60.0	60.0	60.0	60.0
Average Units (AVU) (Above 60)	60.8	60.9	61.0	61.3	61.4	62.0
	62.1	65.3	65.7	66.6	66.7	67.0
	67.1	67.1	67.6	68.1	68.2	68.6
	69.4	69.8	70.9	71.0	71.6	71.6
	72.3	72.9	74.6	75.0	75.5	75.7
	77.4	78.6	79.4	79.7	79.8	80.6
	87.8	89.5				

* Average Composite Rank Index (ACRI) = CRI/N
CRI = Summation of rank indices for nth number of variables
N = Number of variables under consideration

The study report has been organised into eleven chapters.

The first chapter deals with background of the present study, its scope and objectives, study design and study area.

In the second chapter, SSI sector in India is discussed with regard to policy, institutional support, growth and sickness, debate on efficiency of SSIs, entrepreneurship development, and management of SSI unit.

In the third chapter, profiles of sample units are discussed in terms of age, form of organisation, nature of activity, product-type, and size of investment, employment and turnover.

In the fourth chapter, background profiles of sample entrepreneurs are discussed in terms of age, education, training, experience, income and parental background.

In the fifth chapter, the motivating factors, like ambition, compulsion, encouragement, expectation and considerations are analysed. Also, the extent of financial support and other infrastuctural support mobilised from different sources by the entrepreneurs are analysed.

The sixth chapter deals with the operational problems of sample units.

In the seventh chapter, the performance of sample units have been anlayed in terms of annual growth rates of capital, turnover and employment; annual growth rates of capital and turnover per employee; ratios of capital to turnover; and outstanding capital borrowed for fixed investment. This chapter also deals with the factors responsible for varying performance of the four groups of sample units; willingness of sample entrepreneurs to allow the graduation of their units to the medium scale level; and future plans for the sample units.

The eighth chapter deals with the symptoms of sickness of the sample sick units, preventive measures, declaration of a unit as sick, viability studies, rehabilitation measures and cases of sickness since inception.

In the ninth chapter, cases of turning points of select sample SSI units belonging to all the four performance groups have been presented.

In the tenth chapter, regional variations in industrial characteristics and performance is discussed.

In the eleventh chapter, summary, conclusions, and suggestions have been presented.

Growth of SSI Units in the Study Area*

Karnataka State

Karnataka has a long tradition of industrial development with regard to large scale industries as well as small scale industries. Even before the

* *Note*: The analysis in this section is based on unpublished data obtained from the Directorate of Industries & Commerce, GOK.

independence of the country, the State of Karnataka had made notable progress in the field of industrial development. Several *Dewans* of the erstwhile Mysore State, viz., Sir Seshadri Iyer, Sir PN Krishnamurthy, Sir VP Madhav Rao, Sir M Visveswaraiah, Sir Albian Banerji and Sir Mirza Ismail were great facilitators of industrial development in the State (Pattanaik, 1988). However, the growth of SSI Units has been very impressive during the post-independence period, particularly after 1969.

Number of Registered SSI Units

The Karnataka State has witnessed a phenomenal growth of SSIs since 1969-70. In the year 1969-70, there were only 3,900 registered SSI units in Karnataka. The number of registered SSI units increased to 15,313 in 1974-75, 24,851 in 1979-80, and 52,713 in 1984-85. Thus, there was a thirteen fold increase in the number of SSI units within a period of 15 years. By the end of year 1988-89, the number of registered SSI units had gone up to 95,867, recording an increase of 82 per cent within a period of four years.

Investment in SSI Units

The registered SSI units had a cumulative investment of Rs. 34.57 crores in the year 1969-70. It increased to Rs. 105.68 crores in 1974-75; Rs. 199.15 crores in 1979-80; and Rs. 468.84 crores in 1984-85. Thus, there was almost fourteen fold increase in investment in the registered SSI units within a period of 15 years. By the end of year 1988-89, the investment in the SSI units had gone up to Rs. 857.77 crores, recording an increase of 83 per cent within a period of four years.

Employment in SSI Units

In the year 1969-70, 47,960 persons were employed in the registered SSI units in the State. The cumulative number of persons employed in such units had gone up to 2,13,940 in 1973-74, 3,18,284 in 1979-80, and 4,82,443 in 1984-85. Thus, the number of persons employed in the registered SSI units had increased 10 fold within a period of 15 years. By the end of year 1988-89, the number of persons employed had gone up to 7,03,073, recording an increase of 46 per cent within a period of foui years.

Thus, the growth of SSI Units in Karnataka has been impressive with regard to the number of registered units, investment and also employment. However, the growth of employment has been relatively small in comparison to that of the number of units and investment. The growth of units and investment have been almost of the same order and, therefore, there has not been any appreciable increase in the average size of investment per unit. The average size of investment per unit was worked to Rs. 88,633 in the year 1969-70, Rs. 88,941 in 1984-85, and Rs. 89,475 in 1988-89. As for the average size of employment per unit, it was 12 persons in 1969-70, 9 persons in 1984-85, and 7 persons in 1988-89. Thus, while the average investment per unit has been almost stagnant since 1969-70, the average size of employment per unit has been declining.

The stagnation in the size of investment per unit over a period of almost two decades, despite a continuing inflationary condition in the economy, and decline in the size of employment per unit go to indicate that the average size of a SSI unit has, in fact, been declining in the state of Karnataka. However, such a trend seems to be unacceptable particularly in the light of findings of the present study. It is possible that there has been an underestimation of investment, particularly with regard to the additional investment made and additional employment generated by the existing SSI units. It may, therefore, be observed that there is need for improving the system of data collection in this regard by the concerned government agencies.

The investment per employee in the registered SSI units in Karnataka was worked out to Rs. 7,207 in the year 1969-70, Rs. 9,717 in 1984-85, and Rs. 12,200 in 1988-89. Thus, there has been a gradual increase in investment per employee. However, this increase can be attributed not to increase in the size of investment, but to the decline in the size of employment.

Sickness Among SSI Units

At the end of June 1987, 5,105 SSI units were reported to be sick in the State, accounting for 3 per cent of the total number of sick SSI units in the country. Though the position of Karnataka was better than other states in the region, like Tamil Nadu (accounting for 16%), Andhra Pradesh (9%) and Kerala (8%), sickness among SSI units in the state is nevertheless a matter of concern (*Economic Times*, 1989)

Sample Districts

Bangalore District, with 20,520 registered SSI units, at the end of year 1988-89, accounted for the largest proportion (21.4%) of SSI units in the State. With a cumulative investment of Rs. 238.21 crores, it accounted for 28 per cent of investment in SSIs in the state. Further, with 1,88,173 persons employed, it accounted for 27 per cent of the persons employed in SSI units in the state. During a period of five years (1983-84 to 1988-89), the number of SSI units had increased by 81 per cent, investment in the SSI units by 70 per cent, and employment by 34 per cent.

Mysore District, with 9,129 registered SSI units accounted for about 10 per cent of the SSI units in the year 1988-89. In the same year, it accounted for 7 per cent of the investment (Rs. 57.74 crores) and 8 per cent of employment (54,930 persons) in the SSI units in Karnataka. During the period 1983-89, the number of SSI units had increased by 151 per cent, investment by 103 per cent, and employment by 115 per cent.

Dharwar District, with 7,844 registered SSI units, accounted for 8 per cent of the registered SSI units in the State in 1988-89. In the same year, it accounted for 10 per cent of investment (Rs. 83.1 crores) and 13 per cent of employment (93,316 persons) in SSI units in the State. The increase, during the period 1983-84 to 1988-89, was 164 per cent in the number of SSI units, 178 per cent in investment, and 272 per cent in employment in the SSI units.

Gulbarga District, with 3,118 units in the year 1988-89, accounted for 3 per cent of the registered SSI units in the State. Further, it accounted for 2 per cent of investment (Rs. 20.2 crores) and about 3 per cent of employment (18,025 persons) in SSI units in the State. During the period 1983-84 to 1988-89, it had witnessed an increase of 209 per cent in the number of registered SSI units, 205 per cent in investment and 128 per cent in employment in the SSI units.

2

SMALL SCALE INDUSTRIES IN INDIA

Definition

The Committee on Village and Small Industries (VSIs) had recommended, in the year 1956, that SSI should comprise such units that had an overall investment of not more than Rs. 5 lakhs in fixed assets and employed not more than 100 persons without the use of power. While the fixed investment in a unit continues to be the main criterion for defining a SSI unit, the size of employment and use of power have been relegated to the background. The size of fixed investment for defining a SSI unit has been enhanced from time to time. It was raised to:

Rs. 7.5 lakhs (Rs. 10 lakhs for an ancillary SSI unit) in 1966;
Rs. 10 lakhs (Rs. 15 lakhs for an ancillary unit) in 1975;
Rs. 20 lakhs (Rs. 25 lakhs for an ancillary unit) in 1980; and
Rs. 35 lakhs (Rs. 45 lakhs for an ancillary unit) in 1985.

Within this upper limit of fixed investment, the SSI units have been further classified into:

(i) village and cottage units;
(ii) tiny units;
(iii) SSI units; and
(iv) ancillary SSI units

based on the level of technology, location, nature of products and size of fixed investment, etc.

Policy

Recognising the important role played by the SSI sector in the Indian economy, all the industrial policies announced since the independence of the country in 1947, have accorded high priority to the development of SSI sector. The industrial policy of 1956, which continues to be the guiding principle, stated that

> "They (SSIs) provide immediate large scale employment, they offer a method of ensuring a more equitable distribution of national income and facilitate an effective mobilisation of resources of capital and skill which might otherwise remain unutilized. Some of the problems that unplanned urbanization tends to create will be avoided by the establishment of small centres of industrial production all over the country".

It was made clear that while the policy of supporting this sector by restricting the volume of production in the large sector and by differential taxation or direct subsidies would continue, the aim would be to improve the competitive strength of small scale producers by upgradation and modernisation of the techniques of production in such a manner as would not cause technological unemployment. The policy stated that the state should give constant attention to the development of SSI.

The Industrial Policy document of 1977 stated that the main thrust of the policy would be of effective promotion of cottage and small industries widely dispersed in rural areas and small towns. It was declared that whatever could be produced by cottage and small industries must only be so produced and within the small sector, special attention would be given to units in the tiny sector.

The Industrial Policy document of 1980 emphasised that while making all efforts towards integrated industrial development, it was proposed to promote the concept of economic federalism with the setting up of a few nucleus plants in each district, identified as industrially backward, to generate as many ancillary, small and cottage units as possible. It reiterated that the policy regarding marketing support to the decentralised sector and reservation of items for SSI should continue to be in force in the interest of the growth of SSI (Planning Commission, 1980).

The policy framework of Seventh Five Year Plan (1985-90) stated that the policy to be pursued during the plan period would aim at rationalisation of fiscal regime to ensure rapid growth of village and small industries. Infrastructural facilities would be strengthened at various levels. Adoption of modern management techniques would be encouraged. Measures for the development and dissemination of appropriate technology, upgradation of skills, improvement in wage level and continuity of employment, adequate and timely supply of inputs, and adoption of coherent marketing strategies in this sector would be taken. Tiny units would be accorded preference for availing of concessions and facilities. The industrial development strategy for the sector would be so devised that it leads to creation of adequate infrastructure and results in dispersing these industries from the developed urban concentrations to the less developed areas (Planning Commission, 1985).

Promotional Support

In order to facilitate the rapid growth of SSI, a number of promotional agencies have been set up at the national level, state level and district level to assist SSI — both in traditional sector and modern sector. These agencies provide a variety of promotional supports, like concessional finance, supply of inputs, marketing support and research and training facilities to the respective groups of industries.

Prominent among the agencies set up at the national level to assist SSI in the nodern sector are the Small Industries Development Organisation (SIDO), and National Small Industries Corporation (NSIC). Similarly, at the state level, there are two prominent organisations, viz. the State Directorate of Industries (SDI), and Small Scale Industries Development Corporation (SSIDC), that are responsible for the overall development of SSI at the state level. The all-India financial institutions, in collaboration with commercial banks and the concerned State Governments, have set up Technical Consultancy Organisations (TCOs) in most of the States. The TCOs provide consultancy services to small and medium entrepreneurs, banks and financial institutions, and also to the State Governments.

At the district level, the most prominent promotional agency is the District Industries Centre (DIC). Each DIC is supposed to provide all services an supports to small entrepreneurs under a 'single roof' at the pre-investment, investment, and post-investment stages. Further, it is expected to prepare an Action Plan for the development of SSI in its district and establish inter-agency development linkages. In order to increase accessibility to their services, the DICs have been opening their branch offices at the sub-district levels. The District Rural Development Agencies (DRDAs) and the Scheduled Castes and Scheduled Tribes Development Corporations (SCSTDCs), responsible for the development of target-groups of population, also provide promotional support to SSI units to be established by the entrepreneurs and artisans belonging to the poorer sections of society and the SCs and STs.

Financial Support

Financial support for the development of SSI are provided by all-India financial institutions, viz., Industrial Development Bank of India (IDBI), Industrial Finance Corporation of India (IFCI) and National Bank for Agriculture and Rural Development (NABARD), State Financial Corporations (SFCs), commercial banks, cooperative banks, and Regional Rural Banks (RRBs).

Financial assistance to SSI units from the IDBI is channelised mainly through the SFCs and commercial banks. The IDBI replenishes the financial resources of these primary lending agencies by providing refinance to them. A new financial institution, the Small Industries Development Bank of India (SIDBI), is being set up as a subsidiary to the IDBI. The SIDBI is expected to take over all the activities of IDBI related to the promotion and development of SSI. The IFCI too provides financial assistance to SSI units under the different schemes formulated by the Corporation. Like the IDBI, the NABARD also provides refinance to commercial banks, cooperative banks and RRBs for providing financial assistance to SSI units. In almost every state, a SFC has been set up by the respective State Governments. The SFCs provide medium and long-term loans to SSI units engaged in manufacturing, processing and preserving of goods, and maintenance, repair, testing and servicing. The financial assistance provided by the SFCs is only for the acquisition of fixed assets, like land, building, plant and machinery for new units and for renovation, expansion, modernization and diversification of existing units. Since IDBI is the custodian of SFCs, financial assistance provided by the SFCs depends largely on the provision of refinance from the IDBI.

There are 28 public sector commercial banks that provide medium and short-term credit to SSI units. These banks are the main sources of working capital. Other sources of financial assistance to SSI units are cooperative banks, RRBs and private banks. Under the Credit Guarantee Scheme of the Deposite Insurance and Credit Guarantee Corporation, banks and other financial institutions, having agreement with the corporation, can claim 90 per cent of their loan-amount in default by the SSI units or the amount guaranteed whichever is less. Term loan for the acquisiton of fixed assets as well as working capital is covered under the scheme.

Financial and Fiscal Incentives

In addition to the institutional support discussed above, the GOI as well as State Governments provide a variety of financial and fiscal incentives to small entrepreneurs for establishing and running SSI units. The nature and extent of incentives vary from state to state, and depend on the size of unit, category of entrepreneur, type of product, and the development status of the district/area where the unit is located.

Reservation of Items

The policy of reserving certain items to be produced exclusively in the SSI sector was introduced in 1967. Since then, there has been a steep rise in the number of such reserved items. The number of reserved items had gone up to 180 by early 1977, 504 by December 1977, 807 by April 1979, 834 by 1980, and 873 by 1985. The GOI reviews the list of reserved items for production in the SSI sector periodically in order to ensure that the production of these items in the sector is economical and of acceptable quality. Also, new items capable of being produced in the SSI sector are identified and accordingly the list of reserved items is amplified. In order to provide marketing support to the SSI sector, the GOI has reserved a number of SSI products for exclusive purchase under the GOI purchase scheme. The number of such reserved items was 353 in 1980 and it went up to 404 in 1985. Some of the State Governments too reserve a number of SSI products for exclusive purchase under their purchase schemes. A few years back, the number of such reserved products was 185 in Andhra Pradesh, 29 in Assam, 241 each in Gujarat and Himachal Pradesh, 51 in Karnataka and 87 in Rajasthan (Planning Commission, 1985 and Srivastava, 1981).

Industrial Estate Programme

An industrial estate (IE) is defined as:

> "a group of factories constructed on an economic scale in suitable sites with facilities of water, transport, electricity, steam, bank, post offices, canteen, watch and ward and first aid, and provided with special arrangements for technical guidance and common facilities" (Alexander, 1963).

The IE programme in India was launched in 1955 with the sole objective of encouraging the rapid growth of SSI by providing them with infrastructural facilities and economic incentives. Some additional objectives were envisaged later on in the course of implementation of the programme. These are:

(i) dispersal of SSI units away from the metropolitan regions through suitable locations of IEs; and
(ii) promotion of ancillary SSI units for large scale industrial units.

The IEs were expected to be ideal tools for an integrated development of SSI as they could facilitate the organisation of common services, like arrangement for transport, supply of raw materials and marketing of products on one hand, and better guidance from promotional agencies on the other. Further, it was expected that the IEs would provide opportunities to small entrepreneurs for benefiting from the experience of one another and the exercise of collective bargaining power by them. At the same time, the IEs were expected to bring about economic development in their areas of operations through their catalytic influence, and thereby, act as instruments of regional development. As instruments of regional development, the IEs were expected to help in:

(i) generation of local employment;
(ii) exploitation of local resources for productive purposes;
(iii) production of goods and services to meet the local demands; and
(iv) the development of local entrepreneurs.

The impact of industrial estates on the development of SSI has been quite positive though not up to the expectation (Alexander, 1963; Bandyopadhyay, 1969; Nagaiya, 1971; Pradhan, 1985; IDBI, 1980; and Rao, 1985).

Plan Outlay

The approaches of Central as well as State Governments have been to induce small entrepreneurs by offering a number of incentives and subsidies as well as various facilities, like credit, machinery and raw materials, industrial plots and sheds, and marketing assistance. Thus, the roles of Central Government and State Governments in the development of SSI have been promotional, and not that of a promoter (i.e. where the Government itself takes the responsibility of establishing and running a unit). The public sector plan outlays for SSI have, therefore, been rather small. Though the outlay for the VSI sector (i.e. comprising traditional SSI and modern SSI) increased from Rs. 42 crore in the Frist Five Year Plan to about Rs. 2,753 crores in the Seventh Five Year Plan, the share of outlay for the VSI sector to the total plan outlay has never exceeded 4.0 per cent mark (Table 2.1).

TABLE 2.1: Plan Outlay for VSI Sector

Plan/Annual Plan		Outlay for VSI sector (Rs. in crore)	% of outlay for VSI sector to total plan outlay
First five year plan	(1951-56)	42.00	2.1
Second five year plan	(1956-61)	187.00	4.0
Third five year plan	(1961-66)	241.00	2.8
Annual Plans	(1966-69)	128.00*	1.9
Fourth five year plan	(1969-74)	243.00	1.5
Fifth five year plan	(1974-79)	535.03	N A
1979-80		289.48	N A
Sixth five year plan	(1980-85)	1780.45**	1.8
Seventh five year plan	(1985-90)	2752.74	1.5

* The actual expenditure was Rs. 126 crore only during the 3 annual plans

** The actual expenditure was Rs. 1971.71 crores.

Source: Desai, 1983, and Planning Commission, 1980, and 1985.

Progress of VSI

The value of production in the VSI sector increased from Rs. 13,600 crores in 1973-74 to Rs. 65,730 crores in 1984-85. Similarly, the value of export in this sector increased from Rs. 852.5 crores to Rs. 4,557.6

crores during the same period. The employment increased from 176.4 lakh persons in 1973-74 to 315 lakh persons in 1984-85. During the Seventh Plan period (i.e. by March 1990) the value of production is expected to increase by 52 per cent, the value exports by 63 per cent, and the persons employed by 27 per cent (Planning Commission, 1985).

Progress of Modern SSI

Within the VSI sector, the progress of modern SSI (excluding powerlooms) has been remarkable. During the period of 11 years, 1973-74 to 1984-85, the number of modern SSI units trebled from 4.16 lakhs to 12.75 lakhs. During the same period, the value of production increased from Rs. 7,200 crores to Rs. 50,520 crores; the value of export increased from Rs. 538 crores to Rs. 2,350 crores; and the number of persons employed increased from about 40 lakhs to 90 lakhs. During the Seventh Plan period, the value of production is expected to increase by 59 per cent, the value of exports by 76 per cent, and the persons empoloyed by 32 per cent (Planning Commission, 1985).

As per latest estimates, the number of SSI units had gone up to 1.6 million; and the value of production to Rs. 85,000 crores. The value of total exports from this sector in 1986-87 was Rs. 3,648 crores, accounting for about 29 per cent of the value of total exports in India. About 10 million persons were employed in this sector. As per the estimate, the annual growth rate, during the Seventh Five Year Plan period, of the number of SSI units had been 8.6 per cent. During the same period, the annual growth rate of production and generation of additional employment in this sector had been 12 per cent and 6 per cent respectively. Investment in this sector had gone up from Rs. 9,800 crores in 1984-85 to Rs. 15,000 crores in 1987-88 (Raghunathan, 1988).

Debate on Efficiency

Though the SSI sector has made commendable progress during the post-independence period, the relative efficiency of SSI enterprises in generating greater employment with smaller capital investment, capital productivity and labour productivity in comparison of those in the large scale industrial enterprises has been a topic of continuing debate

(Subrahmanian and Kashyap, 1975 and Goldar, 1988). The limited success of the SSI sector in attaining the intended social justice on the basis of which the policy support and institutional support favouring the SSI sector are justified, has also been a subject of criticism (Kashyap, 1988).

A World Bank study on small manufacturing enterprises in India has come to the following conclusions (Little, Mazumdar and Page, 1987):

> "We were able to find relatively little evidence of a systematic bivariate relationship between employment size and technical efficiency, however. The only industry in which technical efficiency was correlated with firm size was machine tool manufacturing. In each of the other four industries there was no relationship between employment size and TFP (Total Factor Productivity) level. . . . The absence of a significant relationship between firm size and technical efficiency means that neither a positive nor a negative case can be made for small firms on the grounds of superior or inferior economic efficiency".

It is quite clear from the available literature on relative efficiency of SSI units and large scale units that the availability of inadequte data and the limitation of techniques have handicapped researchers on arriving at firm conclusions in respect of the relative efficiency of different scales of industrial enterprises. Further, the concern for assessing the relative efficiency seems to be misplaced. Instead of being concerned about passing judgement on the efficiency of a SSI enterprise, it would be better and also desirable to assess the relative efficiency in order to identify items that could be produced with a greater efficiency at a particular scale (tiny or small or medium or large). There is nothing wrong in producing a particular item at the small scale level with the same efficiency as produced at the large scale level. In fact, if the efficiency level is same for the large scale as well as small scale, the preference should be for the latter as it has a greater distributive potential.

A comparison of capital-output ratio of a number of industrial products in the tiny, small scale and large scale sector revealed that the ratio of a particular product was favourable for a particular sector and no sector (tiny or small or large) had advantage over other two sectors with regard to all the products under consideration (Jalan, 1978).

Another study revealed that the intensity of output, income, employment and wage multipliers of 18 groups of small-scale industries analysed was not of the same order. The study, therefore, came to the conclusion that within the existing structure of SSI, simultaneous attainment of the objective of maximising output, income, employment and wages did not seem to be plausible. It identified certain groups of industries that were suitable for maximising output, certain group for maximizing income, and certain group for maximizing income, employment and wages (Saxena, 1987). Further, while measuring the efficiency of a SSI unit in the term of output per employee, it would be better if per employee capital is also taken into account as it would balance the impact of capital on output (Tewari and Pandey, 1986).

Whatever the shortcomings of the SSI sector at present, the growing interest in the promotion of small-scale sector world over, the emerging technologies, changing demand-patterns, and economic considerations clearly indicate the increasing importance and bright prospect of small scale industries.

SICKNESS AMONG SSI UNITS

Definition of a Sick SSI Unit

During the last one decade or so, along with the rapid growth of SSI in the country, the sickness in the SSI too has been spreading quite fast. A SSI unit is considered sick if it has:

(a) incurred cash loss in the previous accounting year and is likely to continue to incur cash loss in the current accounting year and has an erosion on account of cumulative cash losses to the extent of 50 per cent or more of its net worth, and/or

(b) continuously defaulted in meeting four consecutive quarterly instalments of interest or two half-yearly instalments of principal on term-loans and there are persistent irregularities in the operation of its credit limits with the bank.

While both the conditions (a) and (b) should be satisfied in the case of larger SSI units, it would suffice if either alternative (a) or (b) is satisfied in the case of tiny units and decentralised sector units (RBI, 1987).

Extent of Sickness

At the end of 1978, the number of reported sick SSI units in the country was only 20,386, with an outstanding bank credit of Rs. 231 crores blocked in them. By the end of June 1987, the total number of sick SSI units had gone up to Rs. 1,58,226 and the outstanding bank credit blocked in them had gone up to Rs. 1,542 crores (Sivaraman *et al.*, 1989). Thus, during the intervening period the number of sick SSI units had increased seven fold and the outstanding bank credit blocked in them about six fold.

The state-wise distribution of sick SSI units, as at the end of June 1987, revealed that there was a maximum concentration of the sick SSI units in Tamil Nadu (16%). This was followed by West Bengal, Uttar Pradesh, Andhra Pradesh, Kerala, Maharashtra, Rajasthan, Bihar, Orissa, Gujarat and Karnataka. These eleven states accounted for about 83 per cent of sick SSI units in the country (Table 2.2). Thus, it is obvious that the sickness among SSI units is not confined to a particular state or region.

TABLE 2.2: Number of Sick SSI Units in the Selected States at the End of June 1987

State/Union Territory	Number	Percentage to Total SSI units in India
Tamil Nadu	25146	15.9
West Bengal	18129	11.5
Uttar Pradesh	16287	10.3
Andhra Pradesh	14064	8.9
Kerala	11805	7.5
Maharashtra	11457	7.2
Rajasthan	8657	5.5
Bihar	7870	5.0
Orissa	7229	4.6
Gujarat	5211	3.3
Karnataka	5105	3.2
Assam	3542	2.2
Delhi	2577	1.6
Punjab	1834	1.2
Haryana	1819	1.1
Others	17494	11.0
All India	158226	100.0

Source: Sonal (1989).

A diagnostic survey regarding sickness in the SSI sector conducted during May, 1982 and March, 1983, estimated that the extent of sickness was about 6 per cent. However, the units engaged in manufacturing alone and in combination of other activities accounted for about 85 per cent of the identified sick units. Industry group-wise, the incidence of sicknes was greatest in rubber and plastic group (13.6%), followed by non-metallic mineral products, food products and so on (DC, SSI, 1985).

Causes of Sickness Among SSI Units

On the basis of a diagnostic survey at the national level, the causes of sickness of SSI units were found to be:

- shortage of working capital;
- non-availability of raw-materials;
- marketing problems;
- shortage of power;
- domestic problems; and
- labour problems.

However, the study concluded that the basic cause of sickness was the imbalance in the investment and financial structure of the units which tilted in favour of fixed assets with inadequate working capital (DC, SSI, 1985).

According to the Rehabilitation Cell of SBI Regional Office, Visakhapatnam, the major weaknesses of SSI units that led to sickness were:

- deficiency in project report;
- weak equity-base;
- lack of expertise for coordinating with various vital areas of a operation cycle;
- lack of proper planning for production, finance, marketing and management;
- selection of substandard machinery;
- weak viability (of project);
- improper costing;
- inability to manage workers;
- difference among partners;
- absenteeism of manager/entrepreneur; and
- taking too much order, beyond the capacity to execute in time (SBI, 1988).

According to a study by SBI, major problems faced by units with unsatisfactory performance were:

- lack of working capital management (69 per cent of units), followed by;
- lack of organisation;
- lack of technical/managerial capability;
- competitive market;
- dependence on one or a few buyers;
- inadequate bank finance;
- diversion of working capital for capital or non-productive expenditure;
- raw material shortage; and
- shortage of power (SBI, 1975).

An analysis of the causes of sickness of 96 units in Bangalore revealed that (1) marketing problem; (2) dishonesty and diversion of funds; (3) poor management; (4) inadequate experience and planning; (5) non or tardy realisation of bills; (6) death, illness and dissension and (7) production problem were the major reasons for sickness (Philip, Tewari and Pandey, 1988).

A number of other studies on SSI units have found the following as the major causes of sickness or unsatisfactory performance of SSI units. These are (1) shortage of working capital, (2) shortage of raw materials, (3) managerial deficiency, (4) marketing problems, (5) technical incompetence, (6) labour problem, (7) problems of quality control, (8) poor quality of machinery, and (9) bureaucratic delay (Reddy, 1988; Ramaiah, *et.al.*, 1987; Mohanty, 1986; Patel, 1981; Sharma and Singh, 1980; Mazumdar and Nag, 1977; Ramakrishnan, 1975; Patel, 1975; and Pathak, 1975).

Rehabilitation Measures

The guidelines to banks for the identification and rehabilitation of sick industrial units by the RBI, in 1976 observed that any adverse trend noticed, in the course of scrutinising the annual/quarterly statements, might be taken as alarm signal and be subjected to deeper study. The banks were advised to assess the situation and come to any early decision regarding the desirability of rehabilitation in all cases of sick units. A time-frame of about two months since the identificaion of a sick unit was suggested for the completion of whole process, i.e., assessing the viability of unit, decision regarding its rehabilitation, and evolving of necessary assistance proposal for its rehabilitation. Also, the importance of preventive remedial actions where a units showed signs of incipient sickness was emphasised (RBI, 1976).

Another guideline, specially for SSI units, was issued by RBI to banks in 1978. It observed that such units as had become sick on account of external factors, like lack of power and raw materials might be referred to the State Level Coordination Committee for the necessary help. With regard to concessions, it suggested that once a unit was considered potentially viable and a decision was taken to nurse it, it might be necessary to consider reduction in margin money and rate of interest, and rephasing of repayment schedule or funding of a portion of working capital finance to be recovered in a phased manner from out of the future cash generation (RBI, 1978).

Unlike the earlier two guidelines, the guideline issued by the RBI in 1987 was quite comprehensive. In addition to defining a sick SSI unit, the guideline dealt with incipient sickness, viability norms, and reliefs and concessions for the rehabilitation of potentially viable but sick units.

With regard to incipient sickness, the guideline emphasised on the primary responsibility of the management of financed unit to inform its financaing bank regarding the problems of unit that could lead to sickness. The branch (bank) officials were advised to develop mutual confidence between the bank and borrowers. An illustrative list of warning signals of incipient sickness to serve as useful guide to operating personnel of a bank branch was provided.

The remedial steps, suggested to be taken by the branch officials of banks, were

(i) providing financial assistance depending one stabilished needs;
(ii) early reference to the controlling authorities of banks if the required relief assistance was beyond the delegated power of branch officials;
(iii) keeping the term-lending institutions, if involved, informed about the units position; and
(iv) helping the unit in sorting out non-financial difficulties and getting the required assistance from government departments, agencies and undertakings.

With regard to establishing the viability of a sick SSI unit, it was observed that it would be for the banks/financial institutions to decide whether a sick SSI unit was potentially viable or not. However, this process was suggested to be completed as far as possible within a period of 3 months from the date of receipt of complete information on relevant aspects from the management of the unit. Norms were prescribed for establishing the viability of a sick unit. RBI had prescribed a package of reliefs and concessions to be extended by banks and financial institutions to the potentially viable sick SSI units under rehabilitation (RBI, 1987).

Rehabilitation Assistance by the IRBI

The Industrial Reconstruction Bank of India (IRBI) provides indirect as well as direct financial assistance for the rehabilitation of sick SSI units. For the rehabilitation of sick SSI units whose individual requirements are Rs. 10 lakhs or less, the IRBI provides financial assistance upto Rs. 5 lakhs in each case under its Line of Credit Scheme (LOCS) which has been under implementation through the state-level and Union Territory-level institutions since 1979. Where the financial requirement of a sick SSI unit is between Rs. 5 lakhs and Rs. 10 lakhs the additional amount required in excess of Rs. 5 lakhs is expected to be provided by the state-level institutions, banks, State Governments and entrepreneurs themselves. The SSI units that require more than Rs. 10,00,000 for revival are provided financial assistance directly by the IRBI (Goswami, 1987).

Rehabilitation Assistance by the IDBI

The Industrial Development Bank of India (IDBI) has also formulated a refinance scheme for the rehabilitation of sick SSI units. The units financed by banks/SFCs/SIDCs and classified as sick are eligible for assistance under the scheme. The promotor's contribution towards the rehabilitation assistance is expected to be not less than 5 per cent in the case of tiny units and 10 per cent in the case of other SSI units of the additional long-term requirements under the package. It is not necessary that the past loans extended by the primary lending agencies to such units should have been refinanced by the IDBI. The rehabilitation assistance may cover, *inter-alia*, margin money for additional working capital, payment of statutory liabilities, cash losses that may be incurred during the nursing programme, overdue instalments agreed to be funded into a separate term-loan apart from the minimum capital expenditure required for restarting the unit (Shirodkar, 1988).

ENTREPRENEURSHIP DEVELOPMENT AND MANAGEMENT

Concept and Characteristics of Entrepreneur

The importance of entrepreneurial resources as a critical input for economic development has been well recognised. While there has not been any consensus about the definition of an entrepreneur, a number of entrepreneurial characteristics, based on research and experience of working with entrepreneurs, have been identified. Some of these are:

- inner urge for achievement;
- capability to influence and lead others;
- being a problem-solver rather than problem-avoider;
- initiative-taker rather than a conformist;
- a moderate risk-taker;
- being open to learning from experience and feedbacks;
- urge for independence;
- being confident of success; and
- flexible approach towards competition and collaboration (Rao and Mehta, 1978).

It is not necessary that a person must have all the aforesaid attributes to become an entrepreneur. However, it is felt that larger the number of these attributes an entrepreneur possesses, the greater would be his winning chances.

It is generally believed that in India people belonging to some business castes/communities and religious groups are more entreprising than the rest. In order to ascertain the veracity of this belief as well as other entrepreneurial attributes, a number of empirical studies have been conducted particularly in the field of small-scale manufacturing activities. The main findings of some of these studies are summarised below:

(i) A study of 50 manufacturing units in and around Madras and Coimbatore showed that the initial entry into industry was open to persons of diverse social standings and ecnonomic positions (Berna, 1960),

(ii) A study of small entrepreneurs in the West-Godavari district of Andhra Pradesh found that all the entrepreneurs were persons with initiative, drive and hard work, though majority of entrepreneurs had neither technical knowledge, nor strong economic base and political connections (Gaikwad and Tripathi, 1970),

(iii) A study of 100 small scale entrepreneurs in Uttar Pradesh revealed that factors like education, age, manufacturing experience and religion were not significantly related with entrepreneurial role conformity. The entrepreneurs coming from non-business families had higher degree of entrepreneurial orientation and commitment than the entrepreneurs coming from business families, business castes and business region. But the latter had relatively more spatial expansion of markets and higher sales (Sharma, 1975),

(iv) A study of 61 small entrepreneurs in Hyderabad and Secunderabad revealed that the most important reason for starting a SSI unit was the economic gain. The factors like younger age, formal education, urban background, experience in industry, high levels of aspirations, risk taking and adoption propensity were some of the characteristics that were found to be positively associated with the quality of entrepreneurship. Other factors, like high monthly income, technical education, being eldest or first-born male child in the family, membership of organisations and need of achievement, etc. were not associated with the entrepreneurship (SIETI, 1974),

(v) A study of 139 SSI units in Gujarat on the basis of the profit performance of different caste groups revealed that entry into industry and success need not be a privilege of a few traditionally dominent groups. Also, the performance and income backgrounds of entrepreneurs were not distinctly related. While relevant experience was found to hold key to the success of an entrepreneur, the contribution of higher level of education in forming entrepreneurial attitudes and behaviours appeared to be limited (Patel, 1981),

(vi) A study of 90 SSI units in the Marathwada Region of Maharashtra revealed that most of the entrepreneurs emerged from the upper castes and also those who had better socio-economic positions in the society. The industrial entrepreneurship was a result of collective ambitions and aspirations of the family. The entrepreneurship in this region was found to be imitative rather than innovative (Deshpande, 1982),

(vii) A study of 125 small-scale engineering units in the Kolhapur district of Maharashtra revealed that caste, education and parental occupation had greater impact on attaining higher degree of entrepreneurial success (Bhanushali, 1987),

(viii) A comparative study of 192 SSI entrepreneurs in Orissa, Punjab and Tamil Nadu revealed that entrepreneurial activity was not limited to particular castes and communities. However, some significant differences were found among the sample entrepreneurs of the three states. The study came to the conclusion that the entrepreneurs from Punjab were likely to be more upwardly mobile than those from Orissa and Tamil Nadu (Taub and Taub, 1989), and

(ix) A study of 108 SSI units in Punjab revealed that specific occupations and family backgrounds of entrepreneurs were helpful in improving their performance. Further, it was found that the caste affiliations were still relevant in the industrial enterprises. The entrepreneurs in low investment group were found to be more successful than those in other groups (Bhatia and Sharma, 1989).

Entrepreneurship Development

The empirical evidences presented in the previous section does not indicate that entrepreneurship in India is confined to a particular caste, community and a religious group. However, one thing is clear that entrepreneurship does not depend merely on the personality-traits of an individual, and social, cultural and economic factors as well as support-system also play an important role in the development of entrepreneurship. It has been found that the personal attributes of an individual can be improved to a certain extent through stimulation and training provided he has latent potential for entrepreneurship. The entrepreneurial attributes of an individual thus developed can lead to the promotion of development of an enterprise with the help of support-system, comprising counselling, training, infrastructural facilities and financial assistance. And in this way, the impact of constraints, on the development of entrepreneurship, on account of unfavourable personality-traits, social-conditioning, cultural-ethos and economic factors can be reduced to a greater extent.

The first training programme for motivation development in India was organised by the National Institute of Small Industries Extension Training (NSIET), Hyderabad in Kakinada district of Andhra Pradesh in 1964. About 52 participants were trained in four batches. This was followed by another training programme in which 26 participants from Vellore were trained in two batches in 1965. The objective of these programmes were (1) to increase entrepreneurial spirit and to improve entrepreneurial skills; (2) to provide scope for self development by focusing attention on the self and self-directed motivation change; and (3) to generate a continuing theme so that the participants could initiate and control change and (Chattopadyay, 1978).

Later on, the NSIET developed an integrated model for entrepreneurial development. This model was first tried in Assam with the focus on self employment to the educated unemployed persons. By March 1975, 320 entrepreneurs, out of 1550 entrepreneurs trained, were reported to have set up their own enterprises. Similar programmes were conducted in the States of Andhra Pradesh, Bihar and Jammu and Kashmir, (Chattopadyay, 1978; and Akhouri, 1978).

Through an entrepreneurial development programme sponsored by the state level financial institutions of Gujarat, 1240 potential entrepreneurs were trained at different centres in Gujarat during the period of April 1970 to September 1973. The training inputs comprised (1) motivational training; (2) practical and field training, and (3) management training. An evaluation of the programme revealed that the performance of trained entrepreneurs of whom about 72 per cent had set up their units, was quite encouraging (Chattopadyay, 1978).

Following these initial Entrepreneurship Development Programmes (EDPs) and their reasonable success, EDP came to be viewed as an useful instrument for widening the entrepreneurial base of the country. Since then a large number of institutions and agencies have come forward for conducting EDPs all over the country. Also, a good deal of sophistication has been achieved over the years in conducting EDPs. Handbooks on planning, EDPs, selection of potential entrepreneurs, motivation training, developmental inputs, business opportunity guidance and special EDPs for backward areas and women entrepreneurs have been brought out. Notable among these are the handbooks brought out by the Indian Institute of Management,

Ahmedabad (1978) and the EDII, Ahmedabad (1987).

Effectiveness of Entrepreneurship Development Programmes

The different approaches for training different target-groups of prospective entrepreneurs by various organisations in India are yet to be documented in a systematic way and their relative effectiveness are yet to be measured at the national level. However, such an exercise was reported to have been undertaken at the EDII, Ahmedabad some time back. Nevertheless, some of the evidences available do provide some insight into the effectiveness of EDPs.

The EDP Wing of Gujarat Industrial and Investment Corporation and the Centre for Entrepreneurship Development had conducted 376 EDPs during the period of April 1970 and March 1986. The EDPs were reported to be effective to the extent of 63 per cent (Patel, 1987).

In 1974, five EDPs were conducted in four backward districts of Maharashtra, and in Goa. Out of the 88 prospective entrepreneurs trained, 31 had started production at their unit or were about to start production, accounting for about 35 per cent. In the years 1976 and 1977, EDPs were conducted in other five districts of Maharashtra. The effectiveness of these EDPs was about 31 per cent (Deshpande and Panvalkar, 1980).

Before 1980, Development Banking Centre of Management Development Institute, New Delhi, had conducted EDPs in Muzaffarpur District of Bihar, Una in Himachal Pradesh and Chittoor District in Andhra Pradesh. About 79 per cent of the trained candidates were in the process of setting up their enterprises till December 1980 (Shetty, Chattopadyay and Singh, 1981).

The SBI had conducted 104 EDPs till 1985 in its 13 circles. About 28 per cent of all the trained candidates had set up their units. An evaluative study to assess the effectiveness of the EDPs conducted by the SBI itself in 1986, revealed that the main motivational factor in joining an EDP was the possibility of getting easy finance, and the common objective of almost all candidates in starting a new venture was to become self-employed (BD Reddy, 1989).

In Pondicherry, the number of EDPs conducted was 11 in 1985, 9 in 1986 and 12 in 1987. The success rates were reported to be 22 per cent in 1985, 44 per cent in 1986, and 51 per cent in 1987 (Srinivasan, 1989).

In the North-Eastern Region (NER), the IDBI sponsored EDPs

through the North-Eastern Industrial and Technical Consultancy Organisation (NEITCO), NISIET and the EDII-Ahmedabad in the years, 1985-86, 1986-87, and 1987-88. The effectiveness of these EDPs was reported to be reasonably good. Further, 3 EDPs had been conducted in the NER exclusively for women entrepreneurs since August, 1987. Out of 135 women candidates trained, 103 had already prepared their project reports and 86 of them had submitted their loan applications to banks and financial institutions (Das, 1989).

From the limited evidence presented in this section, it is obvious that the effectiveness of EDP ranged between 28 per cent and over 75 per cent. While the available limited information on EDPs conducted in the different parts of the country does not permit to infer any trend in the effectiveness of EDPs, it does indicate that the EDPs have become popular through out the country. As the tools and components of EDPs get further refined and the availability of experts and trained man-power for conducting EDPs further increases, the effectiveness of EDPs is bound to increase in future. However, mere improvement in the quality of men and material for conducting EDPs would not be adequate for increasing the effectiveness of EDPs. Equally important are the quality and adequacy of institutional support provided by the financial agencies and promotional agencies to the EDP trained candidates for setting up and running their enterprises. A good coordination between the performance of institutions and agencies involved in broadening the entrepreneurial base of the country and the performance of agencies involved in providing financial and other promotional support for the establishment of small-scale enterprises is essential for increasing the effectiveness of EDPs.

Not much information is available on the reasons for not setting up of enterprises by a good proportion of the candidates trained through various EDPs. The collection and analysis of such information would be very useful in identifying weaknesses in the process of entrepreneurship development and for evolving strategies to overcome them.

Management of a SSI Unit

While entrepreneurial qualities are essential for a person's decision to start a small-scale industry or other business enterprises, it is his managerial ability which ensures the survival and progress of the venture. The application of management principles on techniques have, so far, been largely confined to big industrial and business enterprises. However, there is a growing realisation, in the recent years, that the application of management techniques in small enterprises could equally be useful.

Whether an industrial unit is large or small, the areas of management applications are identical such as planning, project management, budgetory control, management of inventories, production, accounting, manpower, maintenance, quality control and marketing. It is only the scale of operation that differs. However, unlike in a large scale industrial unit where each functional area of management can be handled by a manager or a group of management personnel having special qualifications, training and experience, in the case of SSI units the entrepreneur himself, more often than not, has to perform all the management functions. A study on the relevance of managerial competence in the performance of small enterprises (industries) found that managerial ability of an entrepreneur played a significant role in the financial success of an enterprise though other factors, like experience and financial position of an entrepreneur also contributed to the success (Patel, 1978).

How to combine the expertise of all the management functions in one individual, i.e., the entrepreneur himself, is perhaps the most formidable task in the formulation and application of management techniques with regard to SSI. The formidability of this task gets further compounded becasue of the weak resourse-base of entrepreneur and his dependence on a number of government departments, promotional agencies, and financial institutions for a variety of financial and promotional support.

It is this difference between a professional manager of a large firm and an entrepreneur-manager of a small firm that calls for a different set of management tools and techniques. In the case of small firms, the owner must normally assume a wider responsibility in the basic management functions of control than does the head of a particular division of a very large firm.

> "In fact, this difference in total responsibility has caused many learned business authorities to say that more ability is needed to manage a small firm than to be a specialized vice president of a very large firm" (Steinhoff, 1978).

Available literature on management of small business presents the details of management tools and techniques without considering the feasibility and viability of their applications in a small-scale firm. Feasibility in the sense that whether it would be possible for a small entrepreneur to generate the required internal data, collect external information and analyse them in order to manage the day to day functioning of an enterprise. Viability in the sense that even if a small entrepreneur is willing to apply the prescribed management tools and techniques, whether the cost of application of these management techniques would be economically viable for his enterprise. Besides, there is a significant difference in the functional approach of a small enterprise and a large enterprise in a given business environment.

It has been found that small firms are more concerned with short-term rather than with long-term objectives, with short-term rather than long-term results, and with tactical issues rather than with strategic goals. Day-to-day activities take precedence over long-term planning. The management process in a small firm is primarily an adaptive process concerned with adjusting a limited amount of resources in order to gain some short-term advantage. Adaptive management process is essentially concerned with tactical rather than strategic behaviour, that is, with attempts to mitigate the consequences of events and to exploit the opportunities presented by change. The job of an owner-manager of a small firm, therefore, must constantly be adapting to a changing situation. The role of a small business owner-manager is said to be a fluid and fluctuating role rather than the role that can be adequately analysed, defined and specified on once-for-all basis (Deeks, 1976).

The management process of a small firm and that of a large firm are said to be significantly different with regard to organisational characteristic, authority and philosophy, and nature of characteristic skills (Table 2.3).

One may not entirely agree with the enalysis presented in Table 2.3, but, one cannot deny the fact that the analysis captures much of the realities of management practices in a small firm. However, not much efforts seem to have been made to assimilate these realities of small firms into a conceptual framework of management.

Most of the literature on management of small firms has almost identical contents with slight variations though the authors of these literature do not seem to be unaware of the constraints in managing a small firm. (Frantz, 1978; Scarborough and Zimmerer, 1988; Siropolis, 1977; Steinhoff, 1978; Macfarlane, 1977; Marting, 1970).

TABLE 2.3: Small and Large Firm Management Process

Small Firm	Large Firm
Organisational Characteristics	
Informal relationships	Formal relationships
No-divorce between planners and doers	Divorce of planning from doing
Appointment and promotions often on the basis of birth or personal friendship	Technical qualifications as the basis of appointment and promotion
Everyone prepared to muck-in as required	Precise definition of rights and obligations, duties and responsibilities
Open system of communication	Structured communication system
Authority and Philosophy	
The entrepreneur or Owner-Manager	The administrator or Employee-Manager
Source of Authority	
Tradition (Ownership), personal	Expertise, office
Basis of Philosophy	
No difference between ownership and control	Control without ownership
No conflict between personal and company objectives	Conflict between individual and organisational goals
No distinction between person and role	Very clear distinction between the individual and the office he fills
Integration of work and social values	Values of workplace divorced from both individual and social values
Not sub-serviant to economic goals	Economic performance as ultimate criterion
Nature of Characteristic Skills	
Entrepreneurial	Administrative
Adaptive	Predictive
Diagnostic	Prognostic
Exploitation of change; opportunism	Control of change
Tactical facility	Strategic facility
Pragmatic use of techniques as aid to problem solving	Coordination and control of specialists
Social skills applied on a personal basis	Manipulative skills applied largely on an impersonal basis
Consequences-mitigating decision-making	Event shaping decision-making

Source: John Deeks (1976), p.227

Not much attention has been paid to the investigation, analysis and conceptualisation of management practices in small firms. The rather rare research efforts have been either a descriptive account of management practices in overcoming day to day problems or evaluating the management practices of small firms on the basis of management techniques that have traditionally been applied to the management of large firms (Shivaramu, 1985; Khandelwal, 1985; Hukku, 1988).

Realising the difficulties of small entrepreneurs in the collection and analysis of vast information, some studies have stressed on non-financial indices and a less complex information system (Cohn and Lindberg, 1974).

Further, as a SSI unit has to depend on a number of financial agencies and promotional agencies for financial and infrastructural supports, it is necessary that these agencies should also function on the sound principles of management. The lack of sound management practices in such agencies is bound to have repercussions of the management of a SSI unit. But, the functioning of these agencies is far from satisfactory. A small entrepreneur, therefore, has to face teething problems right from the conception of idea to the execution of project, from the commencement of production to all along the survival and progress of unit. A national level study on SSI revealed that the average time-lag between the application and sanction of term-loan for a SSI unit was 20 weeks, electricity connection 23 weeks, trade certificate 15 weeks, registration of a unit 20 weeks, allotment of industrial plot or shed 27 weeks, and release of subsidy 29 weeks (Tewari and Pandey, 1986). In the light of these facts, one can well understand the time and patience an entrepreneur requires to set up his enterprise. However, not much efforts has been made to understand the problems of such supporting agencies in India and the prospects of improving their delivery performances.

From the brief review, presented above, it is clear that there is a plenty of scope for investigation, analysis and conceptualisation of management principles and practices in the field of small business management and support systems.

3

PROFILE OF SAMPLE UNITS

For a meaningful analysis of the performance of sample SSI Units, it is necessary to understand their profiles, i.e., their inherent characteristics. The profiles of sample units are discussed here in terms of age, form of organisation, activity-type, product-type, investment on plant and machinery, employment, and annual turnover. Also, an attempt is made to see if there is any significant association between some of the individual characteristics of the sample units and their performance.

Age of Sample SSI Units

An industrial enterprise operates in a dynamic environment and, therefore, it has to take a variety of pulls and pressures in its stride. It has to generate sufficient profit for its survival and progress. As such, the growth of a unit in relation to its age can indicate its performance level. It is with this in view that the age of sample SSI Units is discussed here.

Out of 120 sample SSI Units, about 81 per cent were five years or more than five years old which is a reasonable period for a unit to become a self-sustaining (i.e., profit generating) unit. The distribution of sample units by age-group and performance-group revealed that 5 years or more than 5 years old units accounted for:

- 78 per cent in the very successful group;
- 76 per cent in the successful group;
- 84 per cent in the average group; and
- 86 per cent in the sick group.

Thus, the proportion of five years or more than five years old units was larger in the average group and sick group in comparison to those in the successful group and the very successful group. Further, the average age of sample units ranged between 9.4 years for the units belonging to the very successful group and 11 years for the units belonging to the average group and the sick group. The average age for all the sample units was worked out to be 10.6 years. Thus, there was no significant difference in the age of sample units belonging to the different performance-groups (Table 3.1). As such, the poor or unsatisfactory performance of the sample units belonging to the average group and the sick group could not be attributed to their age.

TABLE 3.1: Distribution of Sample Units by Age and Performance-Group

Age (in year)	VSU*	SU*	AVU*	SIKU*	Total
< 5	22.2	23.8	15.8	13.6	19.2
5 - 10	22.3	19.0	31.6	18.2	23.3
10 - 15	44.4	28.6	23.7	50.0	33.3
15 & above	11.1	28.6	28.9	18.2	24.2
Total	100.0	100.0	100.0	100.0	100.0
Average Age	9.4	10.6	11.0	11.0	10.6

* VSU = Very Successful Units; SU = Successful Units; AVU = Average Units; and SIKU = Sick Units

Form of Organisation

Form of organisation of an enterprise means its ownership structure which has important bearing on the management of an enterprise. In a proprietorship concern, the owner-entrepreneur is solely responsible for the mobilisation of resources for setting up of his or her enterprise and also its management. It is the owner alone who has full claim over the profits made by his enterprise. Also, the owner alone is responsible for the losses and liabilities of his enterprise. In a partnership concern, the responsibility for the mobilisation of resources as well as management of enterprise and its profits and liabilities are supposed to be shared by all the partners, at least the major partners. Sometimes, a partnership concern can be ideal as each partner can, on the basis of qualification, experience and expertise, look after specific areas of the management of an enterprise. Sometimes, two or more persons having different type of resources (financial resources, technical know-how, market contacts and so on) join together to set up and manage an enterprise. The same could be true for the directors of a private limited company with slight modifications. However, in a partnership concern or a private limited company, the decisions regarding the enterprise has to be taken with the concurrence of all the partners or directors, as the case may be, which may entail delay. On the other hand, the owner of a proprietorship firm can take the necessary decision on his own. At the same time, an owner of a proprietorship concern would not have the benefit of the advice and cooperation of other persons in overcoming his problems.

In India, where the members of a family and its assets play an important role in the mobilisation of finances for setting up of an enterprise, the ownership-structure is often manipulated in order to retain the control of a small-scale enterprise within a family. The so-called partners and directors are, more often than not, members of the same family or close relatives. Even in the case of proprietorship concerns, the story is almost the same. As such, the choice of the form of organisation is generally based on the consideration of retaining the enterprise as a family concern rather than on the reationale of organisational efficiency. However, an attempt was made to see whether there was any significant difference in the form of organisation of sample units across the performance-groups.

The distribution of sample units by the form of organisation revealed that:

- 48 per cent of sample units were proprietorship concerns;
- 39 per cent were partnership concerns;
- 12 per cent were private limited companies; and
- remaining one unit was a cooperative society.

The distribution by form of organisation and performance-group revealed that except in the case of sick group, the shares of proprietorship concern were less than 50 per cent. It ranged between about 43 per cent in the case of successful group and about 64 per cent in the case of sick group. The share of partnership concern units ranged between 23 per cent in the case of sick group and 50 per cent in the case of successful group. The share of private limited companies ranged between 7 per cent in the case of successful group and about 17 per cent in the case of very successful group (Table 3.2). The proprietorship units seemed to be more prone to sickness than those belonging to partnership concern and private limited companies.

TABLE 3.2: Percentage Distribution of Sample Units by Form of Organisation and Performance-Group

Form of Organisation	VSU	SU	AVU	SIKU	Total
Proprietorship	44.4	42.9	47.4	63.6	48.3
Partnership	33.3	50.0	39.5	22.7	39.2
Private Ltd. Company	16.7	7.1	13.1	13.7	11.7
Others	5.6	0.0	0.0	0.0	0.8
Total	100.0	100.0	100.0	100.0	100.0

The distribution of sample units by the form of organisation and the size of investment on plant and machinery in the year 1987-88 revealed that the units with an investment of Rs. 500,000 and below accounted for 66 per cent in the proprietorship group, 58 per cent in the partnership group and 36 per cent in the private limited company group. The average investment in the three groups was worked out to be Rs. 519,300; Rs. 626,200, and Rs. 11,59,800 respectively (Table 3.3). Thus, the average size of sample units in the proprietorship group was found to be the smallest and in the private limited companies the largest.

TABLE 3.3: Percentage Distribution of Sample Units by Form of Organisation and size of Fixed Investment in the year 1987-88

Size of Investment (Rs. in 000)	Proprietorship	Partnership	Pvt. Ltd. Company	Others	Total
25 - 200	39.7	21.3	7.1	100.0	29.1
201 - 500	25.9	36.2	28.6	0.0	30.0
501 - 1000	20.7	17.0	21.4	0.0	19.2
1001 - 2000	10.3	25.5	21.4	0.0	17.5
2001 - 3600	3.4	0.0	21.5	0.0	4.2
Total	100.0	100.0	100.0	100.0	100.0
Total Number	58	47	14	1	120
Average Investment (Rs. in 000)	519.3	626.2	1159.8	198.0	633.2

Nature of Activity

Small-scale industrial units are engaged in several activities, viz., manufacturing, processing, job-work and servicing, etc. Some of the units are engaged in only one activity and some are engaged in a combination of these activities. The distribution of sample units by the nature of activities revealed that:

- 63 per cent of sample units were engaged in manufacturing activity;
- 2 per cent in servicing; and
- 8 per cent each in processing and job-works.

Thus, 82 per cent of the sample units were engaged in a single activity—either manufacturing, or servicing or processing or job-work. Such units accounted for:

- 95 per cent in the case of very successful group;
- 76 per cent in the case of successful group;
- 84 per cent in the case of average group; and
- 77 per cent in the case of sick group.

The most dominant activity in all the performance-groups was found to be manufacturing and the proportion of units engaged in this activity ranged between 58 per cent in the case of average group and 78 per cent in the case of very successful group. The second most important activity was found to be job-works. The units engaged only in job-works and job-works with manufacturing accounted for 18 per cent of all the sample units. The proportion of such units was highest (31.7%) in the case of average group and the lowest (5.6%) in the case of very successful group. Some other units were engaged in job-works along with the activities other than manufacturing. Thus, the proportion of units engaged in job-works was also rather high (Table 3.4).

TABLE 3.4: Distribution of Sample Units by Activity Type and Status Group

Activity Type	VSU	SU	AVU	SIKU	Total
Manufacturing	77.6	64.3	57.9	59.1	63.4
Processing	5.6	9.4	7.9	9.2	8.3
Service	5.6	0.0	0.0	4.5	1.7
Job-work	5.6	2.4	18.4	4.5	8.3
Manufacturing and Job work	0.0	11.9	13.2	9.2	10.0
Other combinations	5.6	12.0	2.6	14.5	8.3
Total	100.0	100.0	100.0	100.0	100.0
Total Number	18	42	38	22	120

Product-Type

The distribution of sample units by product-type revealed that:

- engineering products accounted for about 44 per cent of sample units;
- electrical and electronic products 20 per cent;
- food and chemical products 12 per cent;
- leather, rubber and plastic products 4 per cent; and
- paper and allied products 4 per cent.

Others, like wood, cement, lime and aluminium products, etc. accounted for 16 per cent of the sample units. The distribution of sample units by product-type and performance-group revealed that the engineering products accounted for the greatest proportion of sample units in all the performance-groups, except the sick group. In the sick group, the proportion of electrical and electronic product was the greatest (36%). No definite pattern in the product-type in relation to performance-group was found (Table 3.5).

TABLE 3.5: Distribution of Sample Units by Product-Type and Performance Group

Product-Type	VSU	SU	AVU	SIKU	Total
Food & Chemical	16.7	9.6	10.5	13.6	11.7
Engineering	38.8	45.2	55.3	27.3	44.2
Electrical & Electronic	27.8	11.9	15.8	36.4	20.0
Leather, Rubber & Plastic	0.0	9.4	0.0	4.5	4.2
Paper, Printing & Packaging	0.0	2.4	7.9	4.6	4.1
Others	16.7	21.5	10.5	13.6	15.8
Total	100.0	100.0	100.0	100.0	100.0

Investment on Plant and Machinery

In India, the size of investment on plant and machinery has been adopted as a criterion for defining a SSI unit. All the units upto the investment of Rs. 35,00,000 on plant and machinery are at present defined as small scale units, and upto Rs. 45,00,000 on the same as ancillary SSI units. While there is a fixed upper limit for the size of investment on plant and machinery in a SSI unit, there is no fixed lower limit for investment. As such, there could be any size of investment within the fixed upper limit for setting up a SSI unit — though a minimum viable limit of investment is often prescribed for different type and range of products. However, the purpose here is not to examine the viable size of investment on plant and machinery, but to see whether there was any pattern in the initial investment in sample units across the different performance-groups.

The distribution of sample units by the size of initial fixed investment on plant and machinery revealed that –

- in 62 per cent of the sample units the initial fixed investment was upto Rs. 200,000 or below;
- in 22 per cent of the sample units the initial fixed investment ranged between Rs. 201,000 and Rs. 500,000.

Thus, the units with an investment upto Rs. 500,000 accounted for 84 per cent of the sample units.

- It was between Rs. 501,000 and Rs. 10,00,000 in the case of 13 per cent; and
- more than Rs. One million in only about 3 per cent of the sample units.

Further, the initial fixed investment did not exceed Rs. 500,000 in any of the units belonging to the very successful group. On the other hand, 26 per cent of the units belonging to successful group and 18 per cent of the units belonging to the average group had more than Rs. 500,000 initial fixed investment (Table 3.6).

The average initial fixed investment on plant and machinery for the sample as a whole was worked out to be Rs. 236,700. Against this, the average fixed investment for the units belonging to:

- the very successful group was worked out to only Rs. 161,300;
- the average group Rs. 288,800;
- the successful group Rs. 262,600; and
- the sick group Rs. 167,500.

Thus, the average size of initial fixed investment was the smallest in the case of very successful group, accounting just for 68 per cent of the same for all the sample units. This leads to the conclusion that a large size of initial fixed investment is not necessary for the success of a SSI unit.

TABLE 3.6: Percentage Distribution of Sample Units by the size of Initial Fixed Investment and Performance-Group

Initial Fixed Investment (Rs. in 000)	VSU	SU	AVU	SIKU	Total	Average (Rs. in 000)
5 - 200	72.2	59.5	57.9	63.7	61.7	97.7
201 - 500	27.8	14.3	23.7	31.8	22.5	316.4
501 - 1000	0.0	21.4	13.2	4.5	12.5	752.3
1001 - 2000	0.0	4.8	2.6	0.0	2.5	1290.3
2001 - 3500	0.0	0.0	2.6	0.0	0.8	2500.0
Total	100.0	100.0	100.0	100.0	100.0	100.0

A comparison of the distribution of sample units by the size of fixed investment on plant and machinery in the initial year and in the year 1987-88, revealed a significant change. The units with a fixed investment of Rs. 200,000 or below accounted for 62 per cent of 120 sample units in the initial year, but the share of such units had come down to 29 per cent in the year 1987-88. Similarly, the share of units having a fixed investment of not more than Rs. 500,000 had come down from 85 per cent in the initial year to 59 per cent in the year 1987-88. Further, while only 3 per cent of the sample units had fixed investment in excess of Rs. one million in the initial year the share of such units had gone up to about 22 per cent in the year 1987-88 (Table 3.7).

Distribution of sample units by the size of investment and performance group also revealed significant changes. While none of the units belonging to the very successful group had a fixed investment of more than Rs. 500,000 in the initial year, the units with a fixed investment of more than Rs. 500,000 in the year 1987-88 accounted for 67 per cent of the very successful units. The lowest change in the proportion of such units had taken place in the case of average group for about 18 per cent in the initial year to about 24 per cent in the year 1987-88 (Table 3.7).

The average size of fixed investment on plant and machinery for all the units, in the year 1987-88, was worked out to be Rs. 5,99,700. The average fixed investment in the case of very successful group being Rs. 1103,600, in the year 1987-88, was found to be the highest, followed by the successful group (Rs. 700,700), average group (Rs. 415,300), and sick group (Rs. 311,300). Further, it may be recalled that the average size of initial investment in the very successful group was only 58 per cent of the same for all sample units. However, this situation had got reversed completely in the year 1987-88. The average size of fixed investment, in the year 1987-88, for all the sample units was only 54 per cent of the same of the very successful group. These findings further strengthen the earlier conclusion that a large size of initial fixed investment is not necessary for the success of a SSI unit. This may be considered as a significant conclusion as potential small entrepreneurs are often concerned about the size of fixed investment for setting up of their enterprises.

TABLE 3.7: Distribution of Sample Units by the size of Fixed Investment (1987-88) and Performance-Group

Fixed Investment in 1987-88 (Rs. in 000)	VSU	SU	AVU	SIKU	Total	Average (Rs. in 000)
Upto 200	11.1	23.8	36.8	40.9	29.1	118.8
201 - 500	22.2	23.8	39.6	31.8	30.0	346.5
501 - 1000	22.2	26.2	10.5	18.2	19.2	726.2
1001 - 2000	33.4	21.4	10.5	9.1	17.5	1432.3
2001 - 3500	11.1	4.8	2.6	0.0	4.2	2541.8
Total	100.0	100.0	100.0	100.0	100.0	599.7

Employment Size

The number of persons employed in a unit is an indicator of its size. The distribution of sample units by the number of employees in the initial year revealed that most of the sample units had only 10 or fewer employees in the initial year (75%). The units having greater than 20 employees accounted for only about 9 per cent of the sample units. The proportion of units with 10 or fewer employees across the performance groups ranged between 57 per cent in the sick group and 90 per cent in the successful group (Table 3.8). The average size of employment for all the samples units in the initial year was worked out to 8 persons. Across the performance-groups, there was no significant difference in the average size of employment except in the case of successful groups, where it was 5.7 persons. In other three groups, it was 10.6 in very successful groups, 9.3 in average groups, and 9.6 in sick group.

A comparison of the distribution of sample units by employment size in the year in 1987-88 to that in the initial year revealed that significant changes had taken place by the year 1987-88 in the employment size of sample units. The share of units employing 10 or fewer persons had come down from 75 per cent in the initial year to 44 per cent in the year 1987-88. On the other hand, the share of units employing greater than 20 employees had gone up from 9 per cent in the initial year to 26 per cent in the year 1987-88 (Table 3.9).

TABLE 3.8: Percentage Distribution of Sample Units by the Initial Employment Size and Performance Group

Initial Employment (Person)	VSU	SU	AVU	SIKU	Total	Average Employment (Persons)
1 - 10	66.7	90.4	73.0	57.2	75.4	5.5
11 - 20	22.2	4.8	16.2	33.3	16.1	15.2
21 - 50	11.1	4.8	10.8	9.5	8.5	29.2
Total	100.0	100.0	100.0	100.0	100.0	8.3

A comparison of the average size of employment in the initial year and the year 1987-88 showed that the average size of employment for all the sample units had increased from 8 persons to 18 persons. The increase was found to be the greatest in the case of very successful group from 10.6 persons to 34.1 persons, followed by the successful group (from 5.7 persons to 15 persons), and the average group (from 9.6 person to 16.5 persons). In the case of sick group the increase in employment was from 9.6 persons to 11.6 persons. There was no significant association between the employment-size in the initial year and the performance level of sample units. (The Chi-square 12.99 was insignificant at 5 per cent level). However, there was a significant association between the employment size of sample units in the year 1987-88 and their performance level (Chi-square 19.35 was significant at 5 per cent level). This may suggest that an enterprise may require a certain minimum number of persons to be employed in the initial year but the growth of employment size in future would be associated with its performance.

TABLE 3.9: Percentage Distribution of Sample Units by Employment Size (1987-88) and Performance Group

Employment in 1987-88 (Person)	VSU	SU	AVU	SIKU	Total	Average Employment (Persons)
2 - 10	11.1	38.1	59.5	60.0	44.4	7.4
11 - 20	33.3	42.9	16.2	25.0	29.9	15.8
21 - 50	38.9	19.0	18.9	15.0	21.4	34.0
51 - 120	16.7	0.0	5.4	0.0	4.3	81.6
Total	100.0	100.0	100.0	100.0	100.0	17.9

Annual Turnover

The initial annual turnover of most of the sample units (86%) was upto Rs. 500,000 or below. The units with an annual turnover of more than Rs. 1000,000 in the initial year accounted for 6 per cent (Table 3.10). The average annual turnover for all the sample units in the initial year worked out to Rs. 273,500. The same by performance group was:

– Rs. 222,000 in the case of very successful group;
– Rs. 147,900 in the case of successful group;
– Rs. 428,800 in the average group; and
– Rs. 296,900 in the sick group.

Thus, the units that were found to be successful in the year 1987-88 had the smallest annual turnover in the initial year.

TABLE 3.10: Percentage Distribution of Sample Units by the size of Initial Annual Turnover and Performance Group

Initial Annual Turnover (Rs. in 000)	VSU	SU	AVU	SIKU	Total	Average Turnover (Rs. in 000)
8 - 500	88.9	90.5	76.4	90.0	85.6	160.1
501 - 1000	5.5	2.4	18.4	5.0	8.5	740.1
1001 - 2500	5.6	2.3	2.6	5.0	3.4	1550.1
Above 2500	0.0	4.8	2.6	0.0	2.5	7466.7
Total	100.0	100.0	100.0	100.0	100.0	273.5

A comparison of the distribution of sample units by their annual turnover in initial year and in the year 1987-88 revealed that about 73 per cent of the sample units had an annual turnover of more than Rs. 500,000 in the year 1987-88 against only 14 per cent of the units in the initial year. The shift was most pronounced in the case of very successful group. While 89 per cent of very successful units had an annual turnover of Rs. 500,000 or below in the initial year, it was almost the other way around in the year 1987-88. The annual turnover of as many as 83 per cent of the very successful units was more than Rs. 10,00,000 in the year 1987-88. The shift was equally strong in the case of successful group as well (Table 3.10 and 3.11).

The average annual turnover of all the sample SSI units in the year 1987-88 had gone up to Rs. 15,92,600 from Rs. 2,73,500 in the initial year. Among the performance groups, the average annual turnover in the year 1987-88 was the greatest (Rs. 43,22,900) in the very successful group, followed by the successful group (Rs. 13,07,600) average group (Rs. 12,39,400), and the sick group (Rs. 3,85,600). The association between the size of annual turnover in the year 1987-88 and the performance level of sample units was found to be highly significant (Chi-square 47.36 significant at one per cent level).

TABLE 3.11: Percentage Distribution of Sample Units by the size of Annual Turnover (1987-88) and Performance Group

Annual Turnover in 1987-88 (Rs. in 000)	VSU	SU	AVU	SIKU	Total	Average Turnover (Rs. in 000)
Upto 500	5.6	16.7	31.6	63.2	27.4	256.3
501 - 1000	11.1	28.5	31.6	26.3	26.5	716.0
1001 - 2500	27.7	40.5	34.2	10.5	31.6	1604.9
Above 2500	55.6	14.3	2.6	0.0	14.5	6801.5
Total	100.0	100.0	100.0	100.0	100.0	1592.6

Thus, the distribution of sample units by the size of fixed investment, employed and annual turnover indicated that there was no significant difference in the size of sample units across different performance-groups in the initial year. However, difference in the size of sample units across different performance groups had become significant on account of the difference in the performance level in the later years.

4

BACKGROUND PROFILE OF SAMPLE ENTREPRENEURS

A SSI enterprise is the creation of its owner-entrepreneur. It is the entrepreneur who conceives it, it is he who promotes it, and it is he who is responsible for its management and performance. A SSI enterprise reflects the qualities, skills, abilities and resourcefulness of an entrepreneur in spite of the fact that a number of external factors too influence the promotion and performance of a SSI enterprise. The qualities, skills, abilities and resourcefulness of an entrepreneur, required for the promotion and management of an enterprise, may be influenced by his past background, i.e., education, training, experience, income and so on. The background profile of sample entrepreneurs is, therefore, discussed here in terms of their age, educational qualifications, nature of trainings received, nature of experience, income, and fathers' or guardians' background. Also, an attempt is made to see whether there is any significant association between some of the individual background aspects of entrepreneurs and the performance of their units.

Before discussing the background profile of sample entrepreneurs, some clarifications about entrepreneurship and ownership-structure are called for. It has already been mentioned earlier that about 48 per cent of the sample SSI enterprises were proprietorship concerns, 39 per cent partnership concerns, about 12 per cent private limited companies, and one unit was a cooperative society. Thus, if one goes by the forms of organisation of sample SSI units, it would appear that 52 per cent of the sample units were owned by more than one individual. Further, it has been stated earlier that ownership-structure is often manipulated in order to retain the control of a SSI enterprise within a family or close-relatives.

In the case of most of the sample partnership concerns, the partners were family members, like spouse of an entrepreneur, his or her parents, children, brothers, sisters and so on. In all these partnership concerns, it was mainly the entrepreneur who was responsible for the promotion and management of his enterprise and other family members' and relatives' names had been inducted as partners to retain the maximum part of profit earned within the family and also to save as much as possible on income tax. In a few cases (about 5%) of sample units where the partners were indeed genuine ones also, it was the main entrepreneur who had conceived the idea of promoting the enterprise and had mobilized the collaborations and cooperations of other partners for the promotion of the enterprise. In some cases, an entrepreneur had been forced by circumstances to convert his proprietorship concern into a partnership concern to overcome the problems of finance and marketing, etc. Thus, generally it was the main entrepreneur who was the real force behind his or her enterprise.

What has been stated with regard to the partnership concerns was true in the case of the directors of sample private limited companies as well, except in one case where the directors did not belong to the same family or were not close relatives. But even in this case, it was the managing director (the entrepreneur) who had conceived the idea, promoted his enterprise and had been managing his enterprise while other directors were mere advisors or were existing for name-sake.

With regard to the sample proprietorship concerns, the legal ownership and the real entrepreneurship were not one and the same in some cases. Some entrepreneurs had set up their enterprises in the names of their wives or children though their wives and children had nothing to do with the conception, promotion and management of these enterprises. For example, a general manager of a large public sector undertaking had set up one of the sample units in his wife's name a few years before his retirement from the job. Thus, the legal ownership of the enterprise vested in his wife who had virtually no role in the conception, promotion and management of the enterprise legally owned by her. Similarly, a school teacher, having good public contacts, wanted his son to go for a professional degree. But when his son failed to get admission for any professional degree, the teacher set up a SSI unit in his son's name so that his son instead of seeking a petty job after the completion of his education could become a proud owner of an industrial enterprise. In this case too, while the legal ownership of the sample enterprise vested in the son, he had not played any role in the conception and promotion of the enterprise, and in its management for the first few years.

In view of the above facts, the background profiles of 120 sample entrepreneurs who were the real entrepreneurs or the most active entrepreneurs have been analysed.

Age of Sample Entrepreneurs

The distribution of sample entrepreneurs by their age at the time of establishment of their enterprises revealed that:

- the largest proportion (51%) of entrepreneurs were in the age-group of 31-40 years, followed by –
- those who were 30 years and below (29%),
- those between 41 and 50 years (13%), and
- those above 50 years old (7%).

The average ages of sample entrepreneurs belonging to the four respective age-groups were worked out to be 35 years, 26 years, about 45 years and about 57 years. The highest average age was found to be of the entrepreneurs belonging to the sick group (39 years), followed by of those belonging to the very successful group (36 years), average group (34.5 years) and successful group (33 years). The average age for sample entrepreneurs worked out to 35 years (Table 4.1). There was a significant association between the age of sample entrepreneurs when their units were set up and their performance, (Chi-Square 18.91 significant at 5%).

TABLE 4.1: Percentage Distribution of Sample Entrepreneurs by their Age at the time of Establishment of Unit and Performance-Group

Age at the Establishment of Unit (in year)	VSU	SU	AVU	SIKU	Total	Average age (in year)
30 and Below	27.8	33.3	25.7	28.6	29.1	26.3
31 — 40	55.6	58.3	57.2	23.8	50.9	35.1
41 — 50	5.5	5.6	11.4	33.3	12.7	44.8
Above 50	11.1	2.8	5.7	14.3	7.3	56.6
Total	100.0	100.0	100.0	100.0	100.0	34.9
Average Age (in year)	35.8	33.1	34.5	39.0	34.9	—

At the time of survey (1988), about 44 per cent of entrepreneurs were in the age-group of 41 and 50 years, 31 per cent in the age-group of above 50 years, 22 per cent in the age-group of 31 and 40 years, and 3 per cent in the age-group of 30 years and below. The average age for the above four groups was found to be 45 years, 57 years, 37 years and 29 years respectively. The average age was found to be the highest in the case of entrepreneurs belonging to the sick group (49 years), followed by those belonging to the very successful group and average group (47 years), and the successful group (43 years). The average age for all the sample entrepreneurs was 46.4 years (Table 4.2)

TABLE 4.2: Percentage Distribution of Sample Entrepreneurs by their Age at the Time of Survey and Performance-Group

Age at the time of Survey (in year)	VSU	SU	AVU	SIKU	Total	Average Age (in Year)
30 and Below	5.6	2.6	2.8	4.8	3.5	28.5
31 — 40	16.7	35.9	16.6	9.5	21.9	36.9
41 — 50	55.5	33.3	52.8	38.1	43.9	45.1
Above 50	22.2	28.2	27.8	47.6	30.7	57.0
Total	100.0	100.0	100.0	100.0	100.0	—
Average Age (in year)	47.1	43.1	46.8	49.0	46.4	—

Education

Distribution of sample entrepreneurs by their educational qualifications revealed that:

- 22 per cent of the entrepreneurs had education up to matriculation and below;
- 63 per cent were educated up to intermediate and graduation; and
- 15 per cent were post-graduates and others.

The proportion of entrepreneurs educated up to matriculation and below ranged between 14 per cent in the case of successful group and 32 per cent in the case of average group. The proportion of entrepreneurs educated up to intermediate and graduation ranged between 55 per cent in the case of average group and 71 per cent in the case of successful group. The proportion of those having education up to post-graduation and others ranged between 11 per cent in the average group and 22 per cent in the very successful group (Table 4.3). It was found that there was no significant association between the educational qualifications of sample entrepreneurs and their performance. (Chi-square 5.12 not significant at 5%).

TABLE 4.3: Percentage Distribution of Sample Entrepreneurs by General Educational Qualification and Performance-Group

Educational Qualification	VSU	SU	AVU	SIKU	Total
Up to Matriculation and Below	22.2	14.3	32.4	18.2	21.9
Intermediate and Graduation	55.6	71.4	56.8	63.6	63.0
Post-Graduation and others	22.2	14.3	10.8	18.2	15.1
Total	100.0	100.0	100.0	100.0	100.0

About 69 per cent of the sample entrepreneurs had received technical education and an overwhelming majority of them (62.5%) had degree or diploma in engineering. Only 2.5 per cent of sample entrepreneurs had qualifications in management and another 2.5 per cent of entrepreneurs had engineering as well as management qualifications. The proportion of entrepreneurs having technical qualification ranged between 60.5 per cent in the case of average group and 89 per cent in the case of very successful group (Table 4.4).

TABLE 4.4: Percentage Distribution of Sample Entrepreneurs by Technical Education and Performance-Group.

Technical Education	VSU	SU	AVU	SIKU	Total
Engineering	77.8	64.3	55.3	59.1	62.5
Management	5.6	4.7	0.0	0.0	2.5
Engineering and Management	5.5	2.4	2.6	4.5	1.7
No Technical Education	11.1	28.6	39.5	36.4	30.8
Total	100.0	100.0	100.0	100.0	100.0

Training

Fifty-five per cent of sample entrepreneurs had not received any training. The proportion of entrepreneurs who had not received any training ranged between 50 per cent in the case of successful group and 59 per cent in the case of sick group. Among the remaining 45 per cent of the sample entrepreneurs, 24 per cent had received technical training, 12 per cent management training, and 3 per cent had received entrepreneurship training. The remaining 6 per cent had received a combination of technical, management and entrepreneurship training. The entrepreneurs who had received technical training ranged between 22 per cent in the very successful group and 26 per cent in the average group; and that of those having management training ranged between 9 per cent in the case of sick group and 17 per cent in the case of very successful group (Table 4.5). No significant association between the nature of training received by the sample entrepreneurs and their performance was found (Chi-square 10.76 not significant at 5%).

TABLE 4.5: Percentage Distribution of Sample Entrepreneurs by the Nature of Training Received and Performance-Group

Nature of Training	VSU	SU	AVU	SIKU	Total
Technical	22.2	23.8	26.3	22.7	24.2
Entrepreneurship	5.5	4.8	0.0	4.5	3.3
Management	16.7	11.9	10.5	9.1	11.7
Miscellaneous	0.0	9.5	5.3	4.6	5.8
No Training Received	55.6	50.0	57.9	59.1	55.0
Total	100.0	100.0	100.0	100.0	100.0

Nature of Previous Experience

Eighty-two per cent of the sample entrepreneurs had previous work-experience before they set up their own units. One-third of sample entrepreneurs had experience in production line, 18 per cent had experience in general management, 7 per cent had experience in marketing, and 3 per cent were experienced in finance. Further, 19 per cent of entrepreneurs had been industrialists or traders, and 8 per cent had been in the government service. The remaining 18 per cent of the entrepreneurs had other types of experience which could not be classified. The proportion of entrepreneurs who had previous work-experience ranged between 79 per cent in the case of successful group and 91 per cent in the case of sick group. The proportion of entrepreneurs with experience in production line ranged between 26 per cent in the successful group and 46 per cent in the sick group, in marketing between 5 per cent in the successful group and 14 per cent in the sick group, and in general management between about 17 per cent in the case of very successful and successful group and about 18 per cent in the average and sick groups. While about 17 per cent of the sample entrepreneurs in the very successful and successful group had been earlier industrialists or traders, such entrepreneurs accounted for about 21 per cent and 23 per cent in the average and sick group respectively. Further, while only 5 per cent of the entrepreneurs belonging to the sick group had been in the government service, the share of such entrepreneurs was about 22 per cent in the very successful group (Table 4.6). There did not seem to be any significant association between the nature of experience of entrepreneurs and their performance (Chi-square 18.91 not significant at 5%).

TABLE 4.6: Percentage Distribution of Sample Entrepreneurs by the Nature of Experience and Performance-Group.

Nature of Experience	VSU	SU	AVU	SIKU	Total
Production	27.8	26.2	36.8	45.5	33.3
Marketing	5.5	4.8	7.9	13.6	7.6
Finance	0.0	7.1	2.6	0.0	3.3
General Management	16.7	16.7	18.4	18.2	17.5
Industrialist/Trader	16.7	16.7	21.1	22.7	19.2
Government Service	22.2	4.8	7.9	4.5	8.3
Others	38.9	21.4	7.9	13.6	18.3
No Experience	16.7	21.4	18.4	9.1	17.5

Immediate Previous Occupation

Immediately before setting up of their units, 26 per cent of the sample entrepreneurs were working in the production line in industries, 4 per cent in marketing, 8 per cent in general management, and 20 per cent were industrialists or traders. While 2.5 per cent of the entrepreneurs were working as teachers or trainers, 6 per cent were in the government services. About 16 per cent were in other occupations. The combined share of entrepreneurs whose immediate previous occupations were in the industries and trade related activities, like production, marketing, general management and industrial and trade ownership or partnership was the greatest in the sick group (82%). It was followed by the average group (64%), successful group (50%) and the very successful group (39%) (Table 4.7). Thus, the proportions of entrepreneurs engaged in the industry or trade related activities immediately before the setting-up of SSI units being significantly greater in the sick group and average group than those in the successful group and very successful group indicated that mere possession of relevant experience was not adequate enough to ensure the success of a SSI entrepreneur.

TABLE 4.7: Percentage Distribution of Sample Entrepreneurs by the Occupation before setting up of Unit and Performance-Group

Occupation	VSU	SU	AVU	SIKU	Total
Production	16.7	21.4	28.9	36.4	25.8
Marketing	5.5	2.4	2.6	9.1	4.2
General Management	0.0	7.2	10.5	13.6	8.3
Industrialist/Trader	16.7	19.0	21.1	22.7	20.0
Government Servant	16.7	4.8	5.3	0.0	5.8
Teacher/Trainer	5.5	2.4	0.0	4.6	2.5
Others	22.2	23.8	13.2	0.0	15.9
No-Occupation/ Unemployed	16.7	19.0	18.4	13.6	17.5
Total	100.0	100.0	100.0	100.0	100.0

Annual Income from All Sources

Distribution of sample entrepreneurs by their annual income from all the sources before they set up their units revealed that 49 per cent of the entrepreneurs had an annual income of Rs. 20,000 and below, 24 per cent had between Rs. 21,000 and Rs. 50,000 and 14 per cent had above Rs. 50,000. About 13 per cent of the entrepreneurs did not have any personal income before they set up their units. While the proportion of entrepreneurs having an annual income of Rs. 20,000 and below was 22 per cent and about 36 per cent in the very successful group and successful group respectively, the same was about 58 per cent and 64 per cent in the average group and sick group respectively. The average annual income was found to be the highest in the very successful group (Rs. 68,100), followed by the successful group

(Rs. 31,200), average group (Rs. 26,000), and sick group (Rs. 24,800). The average annual income for all the entrepreneurs worked out to Rs. 33,900 (Table 4.8). The calculated value of Chi-square being 16.51 was very close to the tabulated value of 16.919 at the 5 per cent level of significance. Thus, there seemed to be a significant association between the economic status of sample entrepreneurs before they set up their units and their performance. The entrepreneurs with better economic status appeared to have performed better.

TABLE 4.8: Percentage Distribution of Sample Entrepreneurs by Annual Income from All Source before setting up of Unit and Performance-Group

Annual Income (Rs. in 000)	VSU	SU	AVU	SIKU	Total
Nil	17.6	13.5	11.1	9.1	12.5
20 and below	23.5	40.6	61.1	63.6	49.1
21 — 50	47.1	29.7	11.1	18.2	24.1
Above 50	11.8	16.2	16.7	9.1	14.3
Total	100.0	100.0	100.0	100.0	100.0
Average for all Units (Rs. in 000)	68.1	31.2	26.0	24.8	33.9

Father/Guardian's Education

The distribution of sample entrepreneurs by the educational qualifications of their fathers or guardians revealed that the fathers or guardians of 41 per cent of entrepreneurs had education up to matriculation or below. The fathers or guardians of 36 per cent had education up to intermediate or graduations, and those of about 9 per cent had up to post-graduation, etc. While the fathers or guardians of 9 per cent of entrepreneurs were just literate, those of 5 per cent of entrepreneurs were illiterate. No significant difference in the educational standards of entrepreneurs' fathers or guardians across the performance-groups was found (Table 4.9).

Fathers'/Guardians' Occupation

The occupation of 25 per cent of entrepreneurs' fathers or guardians at the time of setting up of units was agriculture, that of 31 per cent was business or service in private firms, and of 20 per cent government service. Twenty-four per cent of entrepreneurs' fathers or guardians were engaged in other occupations like law, medicine, politics, accountancy, and teaching, etc. Across the performance-groups the proportion of sample entrepreneurs, whose fathers' or guardians' occupation was business or service in the private sector was the greatest in the very successful group and the smallest in the sick group. On the other hand, the proportion of sample entrepreneurs whose fathers' or guardians' occupation was agriculture was the greatest in the sick group and the smallest in the very successful group (Table 4.10).

TABLE 4.9: Percentage Distribution of Sample Entrepreneurs by Father's/Guardian's Educational Qualification and Performance-Group

Educational Qualification of Father/Guardian	VSU	SU	AVU	SIKU	Total
Illiterate	5.5	5.0	5.6	4.6	5.2
Literate	5.6	10.0	5.6	13.6	8.6
Up to Matriculation and Below	44.4	40.0	50.0	27.3	41.4
Intermediate and Graduation	38.9	32.5	33.3	45.4	36.2
Post Graduation, etc.	5.6	12.5	5.5	9.1	8.6
Total	100.0	100.0	100.0	100.0	100.0

TABLE 4.10: Percentage Distribution of Sample Entrepreneurs by Father's/Guardian's Occupation and Performance-Group

Father's/Guardian's Occupation	VSU	SU	AVU	SIKU	Total
Agriculture	7.1	18.0	31.3	40.0	24.8
Government Service	14.3	23.0	15.6	25.0	20.0
Business & Service in Private Sector Firm	71.4	30.8	25.0	15.0	31.4
Others	7.2	28.2	28.1	20.0	23.8
Total	100.0	100.0	100.0	100.0	100.0

Conclusion

Thus, the analysis of sample entrepreneurs' profiles revealed that at the time of setting up of sample units:

- successful entrepreneurs were relatively young;
- the economic status of very successful entrepreneurs was better than that of those belonging to the sick group;
- the occupations of fathers/guardians of a large majority of very successful entrepreneurs were business or service in the private sector.

The educational level, training and experience of entrepreneurs were not found to be significantly associated with their performance-levels.

5

MOTIVATION AND SUPPORT FOR SETTING UP THE UNIT

Discussion in this chapter is organised into two major sections. The first section deals with the motivating factors responsible for the conception of the idea by the sample entrepreneurs to set up SSI units, and the second section deals with the support received in setting up of the SSI units.

MOTIVATION TO SET UP THE UNIT

The conception of the idea for setting up SSI units by the sample entrepreneurs is discussed in terms of motivating factors. The motivating factors are grouped into five sub-sections, viz., ambition, compulsion, encouragement, consideration and expectation. To elicit the responses of sample entrepreneurs, a set of factors were listed and also provisions were made to record additional factors, if any, not already listed under each of the five sub-sections. The respondent entrepreneurs were asked to give a relative ranking of the factors relevant to them under each of the five sub-sections giving first rank to

* The WRI was computed by (i) dividing the total number of frequency under each rank by the respective ranks of individual factors; and (ii) aggregation of the values thus obtained under all the ranks for individual factors. The WRIs for all the factors in each sub-section were ranked giving first rank to the largest WRI and second rank to the next largest WRI, and so on. With this method of ranking, it has been possible to find out the relative importance of individual factors in a given set without taking recourse to giving weightage which may be subjective or even arbitrary. The same method has been followed in this study for finding out the relative importance of individual factors, wherever required.

the most important factor, second to the next important factor and so on. The relative importance of each factor under each sub-section was determined with the help of Weighted Rank Index (WRI).* There is no specific prescription about the source of motivation for a potential entrepreneur. There could be any number of diverse motivational factors for an entrepreneur. For example;

- one of the sample entrepreneurs was motivated by the desire to secure a better future for his son;
- another one was motivated by the desire to introduce something new in the market;
- one entrepreneur was motivated by the possibility of developing an import-substitution item;
- another was motivated by being witness to some unhealthy business practices in his employer's firm;
- yet another was motivated by seeing his mediocre friends doing well in their businesses.

There is no end to the kinds of motivation for an entrepreneur. However, the initial streaks of entrepreneurial motivation would have to be sustained by a number of supporting factors. The motivating factors, described by the sample entrepreneurs have been grouped into five sub-sections-ambition, compulsion, encouragement, consideration and expectation, for the purpose of the analysis presented in this chapter.

Ambition

Under ambition, the six factors identified were:

- desire to be self-employed;
- desire to make economic gains;
- desire to prove one's capability;
- desire to gain social prestige;
- desire to fulfil parents' ambitions; and
- desire to fulfil other relatives' ambitions.

In addition to these six factors some other ambition-factors, like desire to provide secure future for children, desire to introduce some new product in the market, and desire to develop import-substitution were reported by a few of the sample entrepreneurs.

Among these ambition-factors, the desire to be self-employed was found to be the most important motivating factor. This was followed by the desire to make economic gains, desire to prove one's capability, and desire to gain social prestige as the second, third and fourth most important motivating factors. The fifth position was held by other factors, like the desire to develop import substitution, to introduce something new in the market, and to secure better future for children, etc. As for the relative importance of the ambition-factors across the four performance-groups, the desire to be self-employed, desire to make economic gains and desire to prove one' capabilities were found to be the first, second and third most important factors respectively across all the four performance-groups. The desire to gain social prestige was while the fourth most important factor in the case of successful group and average group, it was the fifth most important factor in the case of very successful group and sick group. The desire to fulfil parents' ambitions and other relatives' ambitions were found to be the least important motivating factors (Table 5.1). Thus, most of the sample entrepreneurs were motivated by their own desires to set up SSI units rather than by the desires of their parents and other relatives.

TABLE 5.1: Relative Importance of Ambition Factors by Performance-Group

Ambition Factor	VSU	SU	AVU	SIKU	Total
Self-Employment	1	1	1	1	1
Economic Gain	2	2	2	2	2
To Prove Oneself	3	3	3	3	3
Gaining Social Prestige	5	4	4	5	4
Parents Ambition	6	6	5	6	6
Other Relatives Ambition	7	7	6	7	7
Others	4	5	7	4	5

Compulsion

In addition to ambitions, a potential entrepreneur may be motivated by the compulsion of his own circumstances. Sometimes, lack of employment or means of livelihood may drive a person to start an entrepreneurial venture. This can be a very probable compulsion in India where there is large scale unemployment and, at the same time, the government and semi-government organisations have been offering a variety of promotional supports for starting of entrepreneurial ventures by educated unemployed youths. Sometimes, even if one is employed or has one's own occupation, it may not be rewarding enough or challenging enough to satisfy a highly qualified, skilled and motivated person. Sometimes, even if one has a sufficiently rewarding and challenging job, it may not be giving necessary freedom and time for social interaction and for looking after the interest of one's own family. For example, one of the sample entrepreneurs, who was a senior marketing executive in a large scale private firm, was fed up with his job though it was challenging as well as rewarding. According to him, the main problem was that he was finding little time to spend with his family. Also a person may be compelled by the necessity of diversifying his economic-interests as the existing sources of income may not be adequate enough to take care of his family or secure a better future for his children, and so on. Sometimes, the very availability of funds may compel a person to set up a small-scale enterprise for making better use of funds. The combined effect of ambition and compulsion may be quite strong on a person to become an entrepreneur.

Dissatisfaction with the previous job or occupation was found to be the most compelling factor for the sample entrepreneurs to enter into industry. This was followed by the diversification of economic interests, making use of available funds, others, and unemployment. The dissatisfaction with the previous job or occupation and diversification of economic interests were found to be the first and second most compelling factors in the cases of very successful group, successful group and average group. Unemployment was found to be the second most compelling factor in the sick group. In the very successful group unemployment was not at all reported to be a compelling factor. The absence of 'unemployment' as a compelling factor in the very successful group and its being least important of all the compelling factors in the successful group means that the entrepreneurs belonging to these groups were not very hard-pressed for setting up SSI units. They could afford to spend the necessary time for assessing the environment, planning, and working out strategies for setting up of their SSI units. On the other hand, unemployment being the second most compelling factor in the sick group means that a good proportion of entrepreneurs belonging to this group might have been hard-pressed, and therefore they would not have been able to spend sufficient time for considering the pros and cones of setting up an enterprise. Also, it is possible that some of them might have done a 'rush job' and its impact on the performance of their units would have been felt later on. Making use of available funds was found to be the third most compelling factor in the average group and fourth in the very successful group and successful group. It was the least important factor in the sick group (Table 5.2).

TABLE 5.2: Relative Importance of Compelling Factors by Performance-Group

Compelling Factors	VSU	SU	AVU	SIKU	Total
Dissatisfaction with job/occupation	1	1	1	1	1
Diversification of Economic Interests	2	2	2	3	2
Unemployment	*	5	4	2	5
Making use of Available funds	4	4	3	5	3
Others	3	3	5	4	4

* Not Reported

Encouragement

Apart from ambition and the compelling circumstances, a person may need encouragement from the family as well as from the society to become an entrepreneur. The process of encouragement can be described as a confidence-building exercise. To a certain extent, the confidence-building exercise can be a self-generating process. A person could feel confident of becoming an entrepreneur on the basis of his own knowledge, skills and experience and also by comparing himself with other successful entrepreneurs. Such comparisons give moral support to a person for becoming an entrepreneur. The self-generating confidence of a person to become an entrepreneur can be further strengthened by extending moral and material supports by his family members and other relatives.

Previous experience of the sample entrepreneurs was found to be the most encouraging-factor. This was followed by the success-stories of other entrepreneurs and acquired or inherited professional or technical skills. The fourth most encouraging-factor was found to be the encouragement from families and other relatives of the entrepreneurs, followed by previous employment. The least encouraging-factor was found to be acquired or inherited property (Table 5.3). The fact that previous experience and acquired or inherited professional or technical skills were first and third most encouraging factor and acquired or inherited property of entrepreneurs was found to be the least encouraging-factor indicated that the sample entrepreneurs got greater confidence by their own abilities and skills than by the financial and other material resources available to them. Further, the success-stories of other entrepreneurs being the second most encouraging-factor suggests that the success of an entrepreneur can cause a multiplier effect on the generation of entrepreneurship which, if extended, on a larger scale, may lead to the transformation of a "non-achieving society" to, what is called, an "achieving-society".

The relative importance of encouraging-factors across the performance-groups was found to be significantly different. While the encouragement from family and relatives to the sample entrepreneurs was found to be the fourth most encouraging-factor in the case of successful, average and sick groups, it was found to be the first most encouraging factor in the case of very successful group. This shows that moral and material support from families and other relatives would have been forthcoming with greater ease to the entrepreneurs belonging to the very successful group than to those belonging to other performance-groups. This may have some important implication in the Indian Society where parents and relatives are generally reluctant to initiate their wards into entrepreneurship. The preparedness of family-members and other relatives to extend moral and material supports to a potential entrepreneur would mean the elimination of conflict between a potential entrepreneur and his immediate social environment. Such support enables a potential entrepreneur to enter into entrepreneurship with greater confidence which, in turn, may enhance his propensity to take risk. This might have been one of the major contributing factors in the outstanding performances of very successful entrepreneurs.

With regard to the other encouraging-factors, while previous experience was found to be the most encouraging factor in the successful, average and sick groups, it was the second most encouraging factor in the very successful group. Similarly, the success-stories of other entrepreneurs was found to be the third most encouraging-factor, except in the case of average group where its position was second. Previous employment and acquired or inherited property were found to be the fifth and sixth encouraging-factor in all the performance groups (Table 5.3).

TABLE 5.3: Relative Importance of Encouraging-factors by Performance-Group

Encouraging Factor	VSU	SU	AVU	SIKU	Total
Success Stories of other Entrepreneurs	3	3	2	3	2
Encouragement from Family/ Relatives	1	4	4	4	4
Previous Experience	2	1	1	1	1
Previous Employment	5	5	5	5	5
Acquired/Inherited Professional or Technical Skills	4	2	3	2	3
Acquired/Inherited Property	6	6	6	6	6

Consideration

Before a potential entrepreneur takes a decision to become a SSI entrepreneur, he has to select an item or a group of related items for manufacturing or processing or assembling or servicing as per the case. Selection of a product is one of the most critical factors in the process of taking decision to become an entrepreneur as the survival and progress of an enterprise depends, to a greater extent, on its products. A product is the ultimate output of an industrial enterprise, and it determines the size of investment, size and skill level of work force, nature of technology, process of input acquisition, marketing strategies and profit margin of the enterprise. As such, an entrepreneur has to very carefully consider a variety of factors in the process of selecting a product. These factors could be the knowledge, skills and expertise of an entrepreneur himself, availability of technological know-how, plant and machinery, raw materials and skilled workers, demand for the product, and profit margin, etc.

Among the factors considered for the selection of products by the sample entrepreneurs, previous employment of the entrepreneurs in industries or trades was found to be the most important consideration. The second most important factor was found to be the easy process of setting up a unit, followed by the easy availability of technical know-how, easy availability of machinery, and lack of competition (Table 5.4).

Other considerations that did not afford any choice to entrepreneurs in the selection of their products ranked sixth, taking all the sample units together. Some of the entrepreneurs of ancillary units did not have any choice in the selection of their products. They had accepted the items allotted to them by their parent units. Some of the entrepreneurs had so much committed themselves to a particular item that they did not feel the necessity of making a rational selection of the products. For example, an entrepreneur had fully committed himself to produce NI-CD battery, which was being imported into India, and he, therefore, did not consider the possibility of selecting any other item on the basis of rational considerations. The same was true in the case of another entrepreneur who was committed to introducing something new in the market, of which neither prototype had been developed nor commercial viability had been established. Yet, another entrepreneur who had expertise in the manufacture of black lead pencil had so much committed himself to starting the very first pencil manufacturing unit in the Karnataka State that he did not feel the necessity of considering any other item for selection.

Such entrepreneurs cannot be faulted for committing themselves to a particular or unique product. In fact, these entrepreneurs ought to be complimented for identifying potentials and opportunities for entrepreneurial ventures and committing themselves to exploiting them for their own benefits as well as for the benefit of society. Such committed entrepreneurs are bound to succeed provided they can afford to be rational instead of being emotional in their approach. However, they often tend to develop emotional attachment to their products instead of having pragmatic commitment to their business.

Such entrepreneurs were found in all the four performance-groups but their presence was the most conspicuous in the sick group, where lack of choice in the selection of a product or an overwhelming commitment to a particular product, ruling out the possibility of selecting any other product, was found to be the first most important factor. On the other hand, the position of these factors was seventh in the successful group, eighth in very successful group, and ninth in the average group (Table 5.4). Many of the entrepreneurs who had selected their products in this way had run into trouble because they had not taken into account the limitations of their own resources, inadequacies of the existing support-systems and the commercial implications of borrowed capital.

The inter-performance-group difference in the relative importance of the factors considered for the selection of products was found to be significant. However, no definite pattern of the factors considered across the performance-groups emerged.

TABLE 5.4: Relative Importance of Reasons for Selecting the Product-Type by Performance-Group

Reason	VSU	SU	AVU	SIKU	Total
Easy to set up	1	5	1	4	2
High Profit Margin	9	10	2	9	9
Easy Availability of Machinery	3	2	6	7	4
Easy Availability of Raw Materials	7	6	7	6	7
Easy Availability of Skilled Workers	10	9	10	10	10
Previous Employment in Industry/Trade	4	1	5	3	1
Related Occupation/ Profession Pursued	5	8	9	5	8
Easy Availability of Technical know-how	2	3	3	2	3
Existence of Similar Industry nearby lack of competition	6	4	8	8	5
Others	8	7	9	1	6

Expectation

For promotion and management of a SSI unit, industrial accommodation, funds for fixed investment and working capital, technical know-how, supply of machinery, raw materials and skilled workers, etc. are essential requirements. In order to facilitate the promotion and development of SSIs in India, a number of specialised agencies have been set up by the GOI as well as State Governments to cater to the needs of SSI units. An entrepreneur seeking to set up a SSI unit may, therefore, naturally expect to get some of the necessary assistance from the concerned agencies. Also, an entrepreneur may expect some assistance and support from his own family and close relatives. Further, by assessing or scanning the business environment, an entrepreneur may expect to secure some of his requirements from the market. All such expectations stimulate the entrepreneurial spirit of a person, and their fulfilment help the formation and consolidation of entrepreneurship in its initial stage. With this in view, information about the sample entrepreneurs' expectations and extent of their fulfilment were obtained.

The availability of plot or shed in an industrial estate was found to be most expected requirement. This was followed by:

- the expectation of availability of institutional finance;
- finance from family, relatives and friends;
- ancillary relationship with a large firm;
- availability of dependable partner(s); and
- the availability of skilled workers.

The sample entrepreneurs had very low expectations of technical assistance from government or non-government agencies, assistance from government agencies in the marketing of products, in the supply of machinery and raw materials (Table 5.5).

TABLE 5.5: Relative Importance of Entrepreneurs' Expectations by Performance-Group

Expectations	VSU	SU	AVU	SIKU	Total
Availability of plot/ shed in Industrial Estate	2	1	1	2	1
Availability of Institutional Finance	1	2	2	1	2
Availability of Finance from Family/ Relatives/Friends	4	6	5	3	3
Assistance from Govt. Agency in supply of Machinery	8	10	8	10	9
Assistance from Govt. Agency in supply of Raw Material	10	7	9	9	10
Assistance from Govt. Agency in Marketing of Products	9	9	7	8	8
Technical Assistance from Govt./Non-Govt. agency	7	8	10	6	7
Ancillary Relationship	3	3	4	4	4
Availability of Dependable partner	5	5	4	7	5
Availability of skilled workers	6	4	6	5	6

The development of entrepreneurship depends not only on the personal attributes of an individual but also on the society, environment and the support system. It is obvious from the preceding discussion that an entrepreneur expects some financial support from his immediate society, i.e., family, relatives and friends. He normally expects that his society would be able to offer dependable partners and workers for the establishment and operation of his entrepreneurial venture. An entrepreneur expects that his business environment would be able to buy his products. The very fact that the entrepreneurs had very low expectation of getting institutional support in the supply of machinery and raw materials, and technical and marketing assistance goes to indicate that the entrepreneurs were confident that these support could be provided by their business environment. On the other hand, the entrepreneurs had very high expectations of institutional support in getting industrial accommodation and financial resources. The purpose of this discussion is not to dilute the importance of the entrepreneurial attributes of an individual but to stress that society, available support-system, and business environment of an entrepreneur too have important roles to play in the process of entrepreneurship development.

SUPPORT RECEIVED IN SETTING UP THE UNIT

Expectation can be helpful in the stimulation of entrepreneurship. But the formation and consolidation of entrepreneurship would depend on the extent of fulfilment of expectation. Also, the extent of fulfilment of an entrepreneurs' expectation can be an indicator of the contributions of society, environment and support-systems to the development of entrepreneurship. An analysis of the fulfilment of sample entrepreneurs' expectations revealed that the extent of fulfilment was reasonably good. Since it is difficult to quantify the partial fulfilment of expectations, it may be preferable to take into account only complete fulfilment. The overall extent of complete fulfilment of entrepreneurs' expectations was worked out to be 62 per cent. The complete fulfilment of individual expectations for all the sample entrepreneurs ranged between 14 per cent with regard to assistance in the supply of raw materials to 87 per cent with regard to the availability of industrial accommodation (i.e., plot or shed in an industrial estate). The overall extent of complete fulfilment of expectations across four performance-groups revealed that it was greater in the average group and sick group than in the very successful group and successful group. While the overall extent of complete fulfilment was 63 per cent and 52 per cent in the very successful group and successful group respectively, it was 75 per cent in the average group and 65 per cent in the sick group (Table 5.6). These differences in the extent of complete fulfilment of expectations and performance levels may indicate the differences in the quality of entrepreneurship as some entrepreneurs (belonging to the very successful and successful groups) could perform much better than other entrepreneurs (belonging to the average and sick groups) in spite of having relatively smaller extent of fulfilment of their expectations.

Further, there were some significant differences in the complete fulfilment of individual expectations across the performance-groups. The complete fulfilment with regard to availability of institutional finance ranged between 58 per cent in the sick group and 89 per cent in the very successful group. The same with regard to the availability of finance from family and relatives ranged between about 44 per cent in the successful group and about 78 per cent in the sick group. As for the complete fulfilment of expectations with regard to the availability of ancillary relationship with a large firm, it ranged between 37 per cent in the successful group and 73 per cent in the average group. The same with regard to the availability of skilled workers ranged between 37 per cent in the case of very successful group and 78 per cent in the case of sick group (Table 5.6). An important finding was that the assistance from the government agencies in the supply of machinery and raw materials, marketing of products, and technical know-how were not only least expected by the entrepreneurs, but also the fulfilment of these expectations was also found to be the least. As such these can be considered to be the weak areas of existing promotional supports-system.

Discouragement

Once a potential entrepreneur, with ambition and encouragement, takes a decision to become an entrepreneur, he selects a product on the basis of different considerations for manufacturing or processing or assembling or servicing. After the selection of a product, he prepares a project report keeping in view its technical feasibility, economic viability and bankability. While preparing project report, an entrepreneur makes provisions for required accommodation, funds, machinery, raw materials, workers, marketing strategy, etc. In procuring all these, he needs assistance from different organisations and accordingly approaches various organisations with the expectation of receiving the assistance. His expectations may be fulfilled to a varying degree. However, it is possible that even if some of his expectations are ultimately fulfilled to the maximum extent in the process of setting up of his enterprise, he might still have encountered some serious problems discouraging him considerably, causing delay in the implementation of his project (i.e. setting up of the enterprise) or the commencement of production. On the other hand, it is also possible that even if some of the expectations of an entrepreneur were fulfilled only to a very limited extent or not fulfilled at all, they might not have either discouraged the entrepreneur or delayed the implementation of his project or commencement of production.

TABLE 5.6: Percentage of Fully and Partly Fulfilled Expectations of Sample Entrepreneurs by Performance-Group

Expectation	VSU		SU		AVU		SIKU		Total	
	1*	2*	1	2	1	2	1	2	1	2
Plot/Shed in an Industrial Estate	87	6	91	6	94	6	89	6	87	9
Institutional Finance	89	11	71	23	77	18	58	32	72	22
Finance from Family/Relatives	75	25	44	50	67	27	78	22	62	32
Assistance in supply of machinery	17	33	29	29	80	0	100	0	44	22
Assistance in supply of Raw Materials	0	0	17	33	20	40	0	33	14	32
Assistance in Marketing of Products	25	0	0	37	33	17	0	0	15	20
Tech. Assistance	50	33	8	42	0	50	0	0	23	27
Ancillary Relations	43	29	37	37	73	27	60	0	53	30
Dependable Partner	83	0	60	7	87	13	67	33	68	13
Skilled Workers	37	50	40	60	64	36	78	11	49	45
Total	63	18	52	29	75	18	65	17	61	27

* 1 — Fully, ; 2 — Partly.

Note: Whenever the percentage figures of total fulfilment and part fulfilment do not add up to 100 per cent, the remaining proportions account for the non-fulfilment of expectations.

With this in view, an attempt was made to identify the factors that might have discouraged the sample entrepreneurs or slowed down the process of setting up of their SSI units or delayed the commencements of productions, and their relative importance.

TABLE 5.7: Relative Importance of Factor that Discouraged or Slowed Down the Setting Up of Unit/Commencement of Production

Discouraging/Slowing Down Factor	VSU	SU	AVU	SIKU	Total
Delay in Allotment of Plot/Shed	2	5	3	6	4
Non-availability of Tech. Guidance	7	9	7	2	9
Non-availability of Plant & Machinery	4	10	6	—	7
Non-availability of Adequate Finance for Acquiring Fixed Assets	5	1	4	2	3
Shortage of Working Capital	1	3	2	1	1
Delay in Power Connection	3	2	1	8	2
Delay in Water Connection	9	7	9	9	10
Non-availability of Raw Materials	8	8	7	2	8
Non-availability of skilled workers	6	6	6	7	6
Others	7	4	5	5	5

About 38 per cent of the sample entrepreneurs observed that though they had faced some minor problems, they did not face any such major problems as might have discouraged them or slowed down the process of setting up of their units and/or delayed the commencements of productions. The proportion of such entrepreneurs was found to be the greatest (60%) in the avearage group, followed by in the very successful group (33%), sick group (32%), and successful group (24%). Thus, the discouraging or slowing down factors were identified on the basis of information furnished by the remaining 62 per cent of the sample entrepreneurs.

The shortage of working capital was found to be the most discouraging or slowing down factor. This was followed by:

- the delay in power(electric) connection;
- non-availability of adequate finance for acquiring fixed assets; and
- delay in the allotment of plot or shed in the industrial estates.

The fifth set of most discouraging factors were undue delay in acceptance of registration by the parent units, delay in getting corporate license, inability to obtain ISI mark, inadequate orders for goods from the parent units etc. Other factors identified, in order of importance, were non-availability of skilled workers, non-availability of plant and machinery, non-availability of raw materials, non-availability of technical guidance, and delay in water connection. Some significant differences in the relative importance of discouraging factors across the four performance-groups were found. In the very successful group and sick group, the delay in water connection was found to be the least discouraging, and shortage of working capital was found to be the most discouraging factor. In the successful group the non-availability of plant machinery was found to be the least discouraging and non-availability of adequate finance for acquiring fixed assets was found to be the most discouraging factor. In the average group by delay in water connection was found to be the least discouraging, and delay in power connection, the most discouraging factor (Table 5.7).

Problems Faced

About 60 per cent of the sample entrepreneurs were reported to have faced various problems in obtaining techno-economic information, infrastructural facilities and financial assistance, etc. In getting techno-economic information and preparation of project report, the major problems were reported to be lack of data and bankable project ideas. Undue delay and deficiencies were the major problems faced in getting the appraisal of project reports by banks and financial institutions. In obtaining seed capital loan, undue delay and complicated procedures were reported to be the major problems. Undue delay, inadequate sanctions and demand for securities and guarantee were the major problems faced in getting term loan for fixed investment and working capital facilities. In getting subsidies, complicated procedures, undue delay and lack of required knowledge on the part of concerned officials and their unhelpful attitude were the main problems. Undue delay was the main problem in getting allotment of sheds in the industrial estates, power connection, and telephone or telex connection. As a whole, the major problems in getting various facilities from the government agencies, financial institutions and banks were reported to be:

- undue delay in sanction and approval;
- complicated procedures; and
- lack of knowledge and necessary competency on the part of concerned officials.

Financial Resources

The availability of financial resources is perhaps the most critical element in the setting up of an industrial unit. For a SSI entrepreneur, whose own resources are very limited and also who has no access to the capital market, the availability of institutional finances becomes a very crucial factor. An attempt was, therefore, made to study the extent of financial resources secured by the sample entrepreneurs from different sources.

Before an entrepreneur set up his unit, he has to incur pre-operative expenses on the preparation of project report, registration of unit, getting clearance, sanction and approval from different departments, and agencies, submission of loan applications and so on. The pre-operative expenses may comprise the prescribed fees charged by the different departments and agencies, and the expenses incurred by an entrepreneur on visiting different offices, etc. In order to understand the size of amount required for pre-operative expenses and how the sample entrepreneurs had mobilised the required amount, these details were sought from them. However, only 71 out of 120 (59%) sample entrepreneurs could furnish these information. About 88 per cent of pre-operative expenses incurred by the sample entrepreneurs were met from their own funds, and the remaining 12 per cent were met with the funds provided by their families. The proportion of funds provided by the families of sample entrepreneurs was greatest in the case of entrepreneurs belonging to the very successful group (15%), followed by the average group (14%), successful group (13%), and sick group (3%). The average amount of pre-operative expenses:

- for all the 71 entrepreneurs was worked out to be Rs. 9,282;

- for the very successful group was worked out to be Rs. 6,636;
- for the successful group Rs. 12,363;
- for the average group Rs. 7,593; and
- for the sick group Rs. 9,909.

Thus, the pre-operative expenses were the lowest in the case of very successful group and the highest in the case of successful group.

The distribution of funds for initial fixed investment on plant and machinery by the sources of funds revealed that:

- 37 per cent of the funds had been mobilised from the KSFC ;
- 25 per cent from the public sector commercial banks, and
- 4 per cent of the funds had been mobilised from the NSIC, and the KSSIDC.

Thus, two-thirds of the funds required for investment on plant and machinery in the initial year had been mobilised from the institutional sources. The sample entrepreneurs' own contribution was found to be 31 per cent which was greater than the expected 25 per cent of promotors' contribution. As a whole, 98 per cent of the funds had come from the entrepreneurs own contributions and public sector financial institution (KSFC), banks and promotional agencies. The remaining 2 per cent of funds had come from private banks and other sources. The proportion of funds mobilised from the institutional sources (public sector) across the performance-groups ranged between 63 per cent in the average group and 72 per cent in the sick group. The proportion of entrepreneurs' own contributions ranged between 25 per cent in the case of sick group and 35 per cent in the case of average group (Table 5.8).

The distribution of funds for initial working capital by source revealed that while the entrepreneurs' own contribution was 17 per cent, the contribution of banks (public as well as private) was 77 per cent. This meant that the entrepreneurs' own contribution was 8 per cent lower than the expected contribution of 25 per cent, and banks contribution was slightly greater (2%) than the expected 75 per cent. On the whole, the entrepreneurs could manage 94 per cent of their working capital requirements in the initial year from their own sources and institutional sources, and the remaining 6 per cent was met by borrowing from other sources. The entrepreneurs' own contribution was found to be the smallest in the sick group (14%) and greatest in the average group (23%). On the other hand, the contribution of banks (public as well as private) was the smallest in the very successful group (68%) and greatest in the sick group (81%). Thus, the entrepreneurs belonging to the sick group had received greater institutional support for meeting their requirements of working capital than those belonging the very successful group. While entrepreneurs belonging to the average group and sick group had to borrow only 2 per cent and 6 per cent respectively from the other sources, the entrepreneurs belonging to the very successful group and successful group had to borrow 10 per cent and 7 per cent of their working capital requirements from other sources (Table 5.9).

TABLE 5.8: Percentage Distribution of Funds Mobilised for Initial Fixed Investment (FI) by Source and Performance-Group

Source	VSU	SU	AVU	SIKU	Total
Own	27.9	29.5	35.5	24.9	31.3
KSFC	20.3	55.7	19.3	53.5	37.3
Public Sector Commercial Bank	45.7	6.7	40.3	14.8	24.8
NSIC	3.1	1.9	2.8	1.2	2.4
KSSIDC	1.2	4.0	0.4	0.0	1.9
Private Bank	0.0	0.4	1.1	2.7	0.9
Others	1.8	1.8	0.6	2.9	1.4
Total	100.0	100.0	100.0	100.0	100.0
Total Amount (Rs. in 000)	2779	12508	13090	3368	31745
Average Amount (Rs. in 000)	163.5	305.0	353.8	160.4	273.7

On the basis of preceding discussion, it can be concluded that the entrepreneurs belonging to the sick group received greater institutional support for meeting their requirements of fixed investment as well as working capital in the initial stage than those belonging to the very successful group. However, in spite of greater institutional supports in the initial stage, the entrepreneurs belonging to the sick group could make only limited progress and ultimately became sick, while the entrepreneurs belonging to the very successful group could make outstanding progress in spite of having received relatively smaller institutional supports in the initial year.

TABLE 5.9: Percentage Distribution of Funds Mobilised for Initial Working Capital by Source and Performance-Group

Source	VSU	SU	AVU	SIKU	Total
Own	22.2	14.3	22.7	13.8	16.9
Public Sector					
Commercial Bank	53.7	69.9	74.1	80.2	71.7
Private Bank	14.3	8.7	1.1	0.5	5.5
Others	9.8	7.1	2.1	5.5	5.9
Total	100.0	100.0	100.0	100.0	100.0
Total Amount					
(Rs. in 000)	1718	7219	3743	4203	16883
Average Amount					
(Rs. in 000)	101.1	180.5	101.2	191.0	145.5

The distribution of funds for fixed investment mobilised by the entrepreneurs till 1987-88 by source revealed that the contribution of institutional sources (public sector) in the funds raised was 64 per cent and that of the entrepreneurs was 32 per cent. The remaining 4 per cent of the funds had been mobilised from private banks and other sources. Thus, there was no significant difference in the contributions of different sources to the fixed investments made by the sample entrepreneurs in 1987-88, over those in the initial year. The same was true with regard to the contributions of sample entrepreneurs belong to each of the four performance-groups. However, there were significant difference in the contributions of the KSFC and the public sector commercial banks with regard to the individual performance-groups as well as total entrepreneurs. In the case of very successful group, the contribution of KSFC had gone up from 20 per cent in the initial year to 34 per cent in the year 1987-88, and that of public sector commercial banks had come down from 46 per cent in the initial year to 31 per cent in the year 1987-88. On the other hand the contribution of KSFC had come down from 56 per cent to 41 per cent and that of public sector commercial banks had gone up from 7 per cent to 21 per cent in the case of successful group. Similarly, in the case of sick group, the contribution of KSFC had come down from 54 per cent to 39 per cent and that of public sector commercial banks had gone up from 15 per cent to 23 per cent. The most striking difference in the sick group was the contribution of other sources which had gone up from mere 3 per cent in the initial year to 11 per cent in the year 1987-88. There was no significant change in the contributions of different sources in the case of average group. As a whole, the contribution of KSFC had come down from 37 per cent to 34 per cent and that of public sector commercial banks had gone up from 25 per cent to 30 per cent (Table 5.10).

TABLE 5.10: Percentage Distribution of Fixed Investment till 1987-88 by Source and Performance-Group

Source	VSU	SU	AVU	SIKU	Total
Own	31.1	32.1	35.4	24.4	32.0
KSFC	33.9	40.5	16.6	39.2	32.4
Public Sector Commercial Bank	31.4	21.4	42.5	22.8	29.6
NSIC	0.5	0.9	1.9	0.6	1.0
KSSIDC	0.2	1.8	0.3	0.0	0.9
Private Bank	0.0	1.4	0.8	2.1	0.9
Others	2.9	1.9	2.5	10.9	3.2
Total	100.0	100.0	100.0	100.0	100.0
Total Amount (Rs. in 000)	17951	27048	18352	6565	69916
Average Amount (Rs. in 000)	1056.0	659.7	496.0	312.5	602.8

The distribution of working capital funds by source in the year 1987-88 revealed that while the contribution of entrepreneurs as a whole had come down from 17 per cent in the initial year to 15 per cent in the year 1987-88, the contribution of public sector commercial banks had gone up from 72 per cent in the initial year to 76 per cent in the year 1987-88. In the case of very successful group, while the contribution of entrepreneurs had come down from 22 per cent in the initial year to 17 per cent in the year 1987-88, that of public sector commercial banks had gone up from 54 per cent to 78 per cent. Further, the contribution of other sources had come down from 10 per cent to 2 per cent. In the case of successful group, only slight changes had taken place in the contributions of different sources. In the average group, significant changes had taken place in the contribution of entrepreneurs and that of other sources. While the entrepreneurs' contribution had come down from 23 per cent in the initial year to 10 per cent in the year 1987-88, the contribution of other sources had gone up from 2 per cent to 13 per cent. In the case of sick group, the contribution of entrepreneurs had gone up from 14 per cent to 21 per cent. The contributions of banks as well as other sources had got reduced considerably (Table 5.11).

As a whole, while the contributions of institutional sources to the fixed investment had got reduced in the case of all the performance-groups in the year 1987-88 over that in the initial year, there was a significant increase in the institutional support with regard to working capital in the case of very successful ones. In the case of average group, the dependence on other than institutional sources had significantly increased and it had got significantly reduced on the entrepreneurs own resources. In the case of sick group, there was a significant increase in the dependence on own sources.

TABLE 5.11: Percentage Distribution of Working Capital till 1987-88 by Source and Performance-Group

Source	VSU	SU	AVU	SIKU	Total
Own	16.6	16.1	10.1	20.8	15.3
Public Sector					
Commercial Bank	77.5	72.6	77.1	77.5	75.8
Private Bank	4.0	5.3	0.0	0.0	3.1
Others	1.9	6.0	12.8	1.7	5.8
Total	100.0	100.0	100.0	100.0	100.0
Total Amount (Rs. in 000)	17628	17098	11647	4895	51268
Average Amount (Rs. in 000)	979.3	427.5	306.5	222.5	434.5

Comparison of Institutional Assistance for Fixed Investment

The total institutional assistance for the initial fixed investment to the sample units accounted for 67 per cent of the total initial fixed investment on plant and machinery. Out of the total institutional assistance of Rs. 213,45,000, the KSFC and public sector commercial banks together accounted for about 93 per cent. A comparison of financial assistance for initial fixed investment from the KSFC and that from the public sector commercial banks across the performance-groups revealed that while the largest concentration of the assistance from the KSFC was in the successful group (59%), that of the same from the public sector banks was in the average group (67%). Further, the average size of financial assistance (Rs. 2,75,600) from the KSFC was more than double (217%) that of the assistance (Rs. 1,27,200) from the public sector commercial banks (Table 5.12).

TABLE 5.12: Percentage Distribution of Term Loan Assistance for Initial Fixed Investment from KSFC and Public Sector Commercial Banks by Performance-Group

Institutions	VSU	SU	AVU	SIKU	Total	Total Amount (Rs. in 000)	Average Assistance (Rs in 000)
KSFC	4.8	58.8	21.2	15.2	100	11855	275.7
Public Sector Commercial Banks	16.1	10.6	67.0	6.3	100	7885	127.2

The total institutional assistance for fixed investment till 1987-88 accounted for 65 per cent of the total fixed investment on plant and machinery. Out of the total institutional assistance of Rs. 453,42,000, the KSFC and Public Sector Commercial Banks together accounted for 96 per cent. A comparison of financial assistance for fixed investment provided by the KSFC and banks across the performance-groups revealed that the successful group accounted for 48 per cent of financial assistance from the KSFC, the average group accounted for 38 per cent of financial assistance from the banks (Table 5.13). There

TABLE 5.13: Percentage Distribution of Term Loan Assistance for Fixed Investment from KSFC and Public Sector Commercial Banks till 1987-88 by Performance-Groups

Institutions	VSU	SU	AVU	SIKU	Total	Total Amount (Rs. in 000)	Average Assistance (Rs. in 000)
KSFC	26.9	48.4	13.4	11.3	100	22674	527.3
Public Sector Commercial Banks	27.2	27.9	37.7	7.2	100	20720	334.2

was a substantial increase in the assistance from KSFC to the very successful group — from 5 per cent in the initial year to 27 per cent in the year 1987-88. The share of very successful group had substantially increased in the financial assistance from the banks as well as from 16 per cent in the initial year to 27 per cent in the year 1987-88. The share of average group in the financial assistance from both the sources had significantly declined. The average size of financial assistance from the KSFC being Rs. 5,27,300 was 158 per cent of that (Rs. 3,34,200) from the banks (Table 5.13).

6

OPERATIONAL PROBLEMS

Availability

Once an entrepreneur has set up his unit, he requires a variety of inputs, facilities and also demand for products, etc. Therefore, an attempt was made, before identifying the operational problems, to study the extent of availability of different inputs, facilities, and also demand for the entrepreneurs' products. The extent of availability of these factors may vary from one unit to another and also from year to year. Accordingly, information on the extent of availability of these factors were sought from each of the sample units for the initial year and the years 1985-86, 1986-87, and 1987-88. Based on the information furnished, the extent of availability was worked out for each performance-group as well as total sample units for the initial year and annual average for the last three years (1985-88).

It was found that the gap between requirement and availability, as perceived by the sample entrepreneurs, in the initial year was greatest with regard to the demand for products (20%), followed by the same with regard to working capital (17%), skilled labour (16%), transport facilities (9%), testing facilities (8%), raw materials (7%), and funds for fixed investment (6%). As a whole, the extent of availability in the initial year was found to be 91 per cent. A comparison of the extent of availabilities across the performance-groups revealed that the extent of availability was greater in the average group and sick group than that in the very successful group and successful group. It ranged between 89 per cent in the successful group and about 94 per cent in the sick group (Table 6.1). The units belonging to the average group and sick group did not have any major disadvantage in comparison to those belonging to the very successful group and successful group to begin with. In fact, the extent of availability in some cases was significantly greater in the average group and sick group in the initial year.

TABLE 6.1: Percentage Availability to the Requirement of Input Items, facilities and demand, etc. in the Initial Year Performance-Group

Input Item	VSU	SU	AVU	SIKU	Total
Funds for Fixed Investment	91	92	97	97	94
Funds for Working Capital	83	80	87	81	83
Raw Materials	94	92	97	88	93
Fuel	100	100	98	100	100
Electric Power	96	94	97	100	97
Skilled Labour	80	83	81	92	84
Unskilled Labour	95	97	99	96	97
Transportation Facilities	79	90	95	100	91
Testing Facilities	91	89	88	100	92
Demand for Products	82	74	82	81	80
Average	90	89	92	94	91

The gap between the availability of different inputs, facilities and demand for products during the period 1985-88 was found to be the greatest with regard to working capital (22%), followed by the demand for products (17%), skilled workers (13%), electric power (10%), and raw materials (7%). In the case of other such factors, the difference between availability and requirement varied from 1 per cent to 4 per cent. The overall extent of availability was found to be almost the same as in the initial year (Table 6.2).

A comparison of the extent of availability with regard to individual factors for all the sample units in the initial year and during the period 1985-88, showed minor variations. The availability of working capital during the period 1985-88 had declined from 83 per cent in the initial year to 78 per cent, and the availability of electric power had declined from 97 per cent to 90 per cent. However, these losses should not be taken in terms of absolute losses but relative losses. In other words, perhaps the availability had not been able to keep pace with the growing requirements.

As for the extent of availability of individual factors across the different performance-groups, the availability of working capital ranged between 61 per cent in the case of sick group and 84 per cent in the case of successful group. It had declined in all the performance groups, except the successful group, during the period 1985-88 over that in the initial year. The decline was significantly high in the sick group (from 81 to 61%) and modest in the very successful group and average group. The availability of electric power had declined during the period 1985-88 over that in the initial year in he case of all the performance-groups. The most significant differences across the performance-groups were found with regard to the demand for products. During the period 1985-88, the demand for products ranged between 69 per cent in the sick group and 93 per cent in the very successful group. While the demand for products had increased from 74 per cent to 91 per cent during the period 1985-88 over that in the initial year in the case of successful group, the same had declined from 81 per cent to 69 per cent in the case of sick group (Table 6.2).

TABLE 6.2: Percentage Availability to the Requirement of Input Items, facilities and demand, etc., during the period 1985-88 by Performance-Group

Input Item	VSU	SU	AVU	SIKU	Total
Funds for Fixed Investment	95	95	99	99	97
Funds for Working Capital	81	84	84	61	78
Raw Materials	95	92	96	86	93
Fuel	100	96	98	100	98
Electric Power	91	88	87	94	90
Skilled Labour	89	83	86	90	87
Unskilled labour	96	96	97	96	96
Transportation Facilities	93	93	99	100	96
Testing Facilities	96	93	97	100	96
Demand for Products	93	91	80	69	83
Average	93	91	92	90	91

Major Problems

On the basis of mere availability of certain inputs, facilities, and the demand for products to a greater extent to an entrepreneur, it cannot be said that he does not have any operational problem. It is possible that even if an entrepreneur has been getting adequate supply of raw materials, the quality may not be of required standard or the costs may be high. Similarly, even if there is adequate supply of electricity, the cost of electricity may be high or the supply may not be reliable because of frequent power-cuts. Further, even if there is adequate supply of skilled workers, they may not be available at reasonable wages and salary or there may be absenteeism or job-hopping or trade unionism, etc. Thus, even if there is adequate supply of certain inputs there may be some operational problems with regard to the same. On the other hand, even if there are shortages of certain inputs they may not be causing major operational problems. With this in view, the details of operational problems faced by the entrepreneurs in the initial year and in the years 1985-1988 were sought from them in order of importance. The relative importance of individual problems was determined for the two periods, initial year and the period 1985-1988. About 90 per cent of the sample entrepreneurs had reported a number of operational problems.

In the initial year, marketing problems were found to be the most difficult ones. This was followed by the shortage of working capital, labour problems, inadequacy of capital for fixed investment, power supply problem, and problems in the supply of raw materials. Other major problems in order of importance were with regard to government policies and rules, statutory obligations, lack of water supply, management problems, obsolete technology, transportation problems, and lack of technical and consultancy services. A comparison of problems faced by the sample entrepreneurs belonging to the four performance-groups revealed that marketing of products and the shortage of working capital were the first two most difficult problems in all the groups. Labour problems were found to be the third most difficult problems except in the case of sick group where it was the sixth most difficult problem. As a whole, there did not emerge any pattern in the operational problems faced by the entrepreneurs belonging to the four performance-groups during the initial year (Table 6.3).

During the period 1985-88, the shortage of working capital was found to be the most difficult problem. This was followed by labour problem, marketing problem, and power (electricity) supply problem. The fifth most difficult problem was found to be the government policies and rules, followed by the raw material problem, water supply problem, problems on account of statutory obligations, inadequacy of capital for fixed investment, and management problems. Other problems faced, in order to importance, were obsolete technology, transportation problems, and lack of technical and consultancy services. Thus, some significant shifts had taken place in the relative importance of problems during the period 1985-88 over that in the initial year (Table 6.3). For example, marketing problem was the first most difficult problem in the initial year but its position had shifted to the third most difficult problem during the period 1985-88. On the other hand, the working capital problem and labour problem, which were second and third most difficult problems respectively in the initial year, had become first and second most difficult problems respectively during the period 1985-88. The power supply problem had shifted from fifth to the fourth position and the inadequacy of capital for fixed investment from fourth to eighth position. While the relative importance of raw materials remained same in the initial year as well as during the period 1985-88, that of the government policies had shifted from seventh to the fifth position. Thus, while the problems on account of marketing and inadequacy of capital for fixed investment had become less acute, the same on account of the shortage of working capital, power supply, labour, and government policies had become relatively more acute.

A comparison of the relative importance of problems during the period 1985-88, across the performance-groups, did not reveal any clear-cut pattern except in the case of power supply problem (Table 6.3).

TABLE 6.3: Relative Importance of Operational Problems faced by Sample Units during the Initial Year and the period 1985-88 by Performance-Group

Operational Problem	VSU		SU		AVU		SIKU		Total	
	1*	2*	1	2	1	2	1	2	1	2
Capital for Fixed Investment	5	9	4	9	7	9	4	—	4	8
Working Capital	2	1	1	2	2	1	2	1	2	1
Water Supply	10	7	9	8	6	6	9	7	9	7
Power Supply	6	5	5	5	4	4	8	4	5	4
Labour	3	6	3	1	3	3	6	5	3	2
Raw Material	4	4	8	7	7	5	3	3	6	6
Marketing	1	2	2	4	1	2	1	2	1	3
Transportation	12	11	10	11	—	13	10	—	12	12
ObsoleteTechnology	12	12	11	12	9	10	—	—	11	11
Management	9	8	12	10	—	11	7	8	10	10
Technical & Consultant Services	8	12	13	13	10	12	10	—	13	8
Govt. Policy and Rules	7	3	7	3	5	8	5	6	7	5
Statutory Obligations	11	10	6	6	8	7	10	—	8	8

*1 — Initial year; 2 — 1985-88

Note: Ranks based on weighted Rank Index.

Nature of Major Operational Problems

Raw Material Problem

Among the problems related to raw materials, the scarcity of raw materials was found to be the most difficult problem in the initial year, followed by the high costs of raw materials, lack of the supply of critical inputs from the parent unit (in the case of ancillary units), non-availability of raw materials in the required quantity, i.e., raw materials could be bought only in the quantities prescribed by the suppliers and not as required by the entrepreneurs. The fourth and fifth problems were poor quality of raw materials and transportation problems respectively (Table 6.4).

During the period 1985-88, the high cost of raw materials was found to be the most difficult problem, followed by the scarcity of raw materials and poor quality of raw materials. Other problems, as discussed in the preceding paragraph, were found to be the fourth problems (Table 6.4).

TABLE 6.4: Relative Importance of the Nature of Raw Material Problems Faced by Sample Units in the Initial Year and the period 1985-88 by Performance-Group

Nature of Raw Material Problem	VSU		SU		AVU		SIKU		Total	
	1*	2*	1	2	1	2	1	2	1	2
Scarcity	1	1	2	2	2	3	1	1	1	2
Poor Quality	4	4	4	3	1	1	—	4	4	3
High Cost	2	2	1	1	3	2	3	2	2	1
Transportation Problem	5	5	3	4	4	5	—	5	5	5
Others	3	3	5	5	—	4	2	3	3	4

* 1 — Initial year; 2 — 1985-88

Power Supply Problem

Adequate and uninterrupted supply of electric power is essential for the efficient operation of a SSI unit. Many of the sample entrepreneurs complained that apart from inadequate supply of power to their units, frequent power-cuts affected the performance of their units as their workers had to idle their time on duty during the period of power-cuts.

Also, because of the inconvenient load-shedding schedules they were finding it difficult to programme their production-schedules. Sometimes, the low-voltage of power supplied too affected production at their units. While the inadequacy and unreliability of power supply had increased over the years, the rates of electricity charges were being raised year after year.

During the initial year, the inadequacy of power supply was found to be the most difficult problem. This was followed by uncertainty of the supply, and high cost.

TABLE 6.5: Relative Importance of the Nature of Power (Electric) Problem faced by Sample Units in the Initial Year and the period 1985-88 by Performance-Group

Nature of Electric Power Problem	VSU		SU		AVU		SIKU		Total	
	1*	2*	1	2	1	2	1	2	1	2
Inadequacy	2	1	1	2	1	2	1	1	1	1
Uncertainty	1	2	2	1	2	1	—	3	2	2
High Cost	3	3	—	3	3	3	—	2	3	3

* 1 — Initial Year; 2 — 1985-88

The impact of power supply problems appeared to be very limited in the case of sick group during the initial year (Table 6.5).

The relative importance of the different types of power supply problem continued to be in the same order during the period 1985-88 as in the initial year (Table 6.5). From the relative importance of the three types of power supply problems in the initial year as well as during 1985-88, it is obvious that the entrepreneurs were not so much concerned about the high cost as about the inadequacy and uncertainty of power supply.

Marketing Problem

Marketing problem was found to be one of the most difficult problems faced by the sample entrepreneurs across all the performance-groups. Among the nature of marketing problems faced by the sample entrepreneurs in the initial year, the problems, like inadequate and irregular order from the parent units, lack of ISI mark, and stiff competition due to imports, grouped as others, were found to be the most difficult problems. The second most difficult marketing problem in the initial year was found to be the demand on credit, followed by the competition from SSI units, long distance scattered demand, slackness in demand, and competition from large scale industrial units. The seasonal demand was found to be the least difficult problem. Competition from the SSI units was found to be the most difficult problem in the very successful group, followed by the slackness in demand and other marketing problems as listed above. In the successful group, the most difficult problem was found to be the demand on credit, followed by the slackness in demand, and long distance scattered demand. In the average group, other marketing problems, as listed above, were found to be the most difficult ones, followed by the demand on credit, and competition from the SSI units. In the sick group, again the other problems, as listed above, were found to be the most difficult problems, followed by seasonal demand, demand on credit, and competition from the SSI units (Table 6.6). Thus, while the greatest concern of the very successful entrepreneurs in the marketing of their products, in the initial year, was the competition with other SSI units, and the greatest concern of successful entrepreneurs was the marketing of their products on credit basis, the greatest concern of the entrepreneurs belonging to the average group and sick group was of not getting adequate order from the large scale units, etc.

During the period 1985-88, the demand on credit was found to be the most difficult marketing problem, followed by the competition from other SSI units, slackness in demand, other problems (listed earlier), long distance scattered demand, and competition from large units. The seasonal demand was again found to be the least important (Table 6.7). While the relative importance of demand on credit, competition from other SSI units, and slackness in demand had become greater during the period 1985-88 over that in the initial year, the same of the long distance scattered demand and other marketing problems had gone down. The competition from large sacle units being the sixth most difficult problem in the initial year and the fifth most difficult problem during the period 1985-88 indicated that the sample entrepreneurs did not consider it a major marketing problem. On the other hand, the competition from other SSI units appeared to be a much more formidable marketing problem as it was found to be the third most difficult problem in the initial year and the second most difficult problem during the period 1985-88. An important problem faced by entrepreneurs belonging to the sick group was that some of them had lost their old customers due to the closure of their (sample entrepreneurs') units in past and were finding it difficult to recapture them again.

TABLE 6.6: Relative Importance of the Nature of Marketing Problems faced by Sample Units in the initial Year and the Period 1985-88 by Performance-Group

Nature of Marketing Problem	VSU		SU		AVU		SIKU		Total	
	1*	2*	1	2	1	2	1	2	1	2
Competition from other SSI units	1	3	6	1	2	1	3	3	3	2
Competition from Large Scale Units	6	3	5	6	7	7	5	5	6	5
Slackness in Demand	2	6	2	3	6	5	7	4	5	3
Seasonal Demand	—	7	7	7	4	4	2	6	7	7
Demand on Credit	4	2	1	2	2	2	3	2	2	1
Long Distance Scattered Demand	5	5	3	5	5	6	5	7	4	5
Others	3	1	4	4	1	3	1	1	1	4

* 1 — Initial year; 2 — 1985-88

The demand on credit was found to be the first most difficult problem for all the sample units, and the second most difficult problem in all the four performance-groups. Marketing of products on credit basis is not an unusual marketing practice. Such a marketing strategy cannot be a major problem provided the customers make payments within a reasonable period, mutually accepted by the customers and entrepreneurs. But, when payments are inordinately delayed by the customers, the inordinate delay generates a chain of adverse reactions affecting the performance of a SSI unit. The inordinate delay in payments results in the shortage of working capital which may lead to the delay in payment to workers and suppliers and the entrepreneur may lose the good-will of both which would hamper the execution of other orders received. Also, there is a likely danger of the relationship of entrepreneurs with their bankers getting strained on account of default or delay in making repayments to banks. Further, the cost of capital may also increase if an entrepreneur is not able to make repayments to his or her financing agency on one hand and the idling of borrowed capital because of the delayed payments by the customers on the other. In this process, a SSI entrepreneur becomes a net financier to customers while in some of the developed countries it is the large scale enterprises who are the net financiers to SSI units. The problems related to the marketing of products on credit basis were reported by a large number of sample entrepreneurs. At the same time, they stated that they could not avoid this practice because of stiff competition with other SSI units.

Labour Problems

In the initial year, the lack of skilled workers was found to be the most difficult labour problem. The second most difficult problem was job-hopping by workers, followed by absenteeism. The fourth most difficult problem was found to be the lack of training facility for workers. A large number of sample entrepreneurs observed that because of the lack of training facilities for workers, there was a shortage of skilled workers. The entrepreneurs had, therefore, to recruit unskilled workers and train them for a few months to effectively employ them. However, once a worker had received training and learnt the required skills, he demanded higher salary or wages and if the entrepreneur was not in a position to pay the demanded salary/wage, the worker would generally look for job in some other unit. The trade unionism was found to be the least difficult problem faced by the sample entrepreneurs (Table 6.7).

TABLE 6.7: Relative Importance of the Nature of Labour Problem Faced by Sample Units in the Initial year and the period 1985-88 by Performance-Group

Nature of Labour Problem	VSU		SU		AVU		SIKU		Total	
	1*	2*	1	2	1	2	1	2	1	2
Lack of Skilled Worker	1	1	1	1	1	1	2	1	1	1
Lack of Training Facility	4	4	2	4	4	5	4	5	4	4
Trade Unionism	5	5	6	5	5	4	—	3	5	5
Absenteeism	2	2	3	3	3	3	1	2	3	2
Job-hopping	3	3	4	2	2	2	3	4	2	3

* 1 — Initial year; 2 — 1985-88

During the period 1985-88, the relative importance of the nature of labour problems remained almost in the same order as in the initial year (Table 6.7).

Labour Law Problem

In order to ensure the welfare of industrial workers, the government had made certain rules to be observed by the employers. As per these rules, a worker is entitled to get minimum salary or wage, minimum bonus, Employees State Insurance (ESI) facility and provident funds, etc. if the unit, where he or she is working, comes under the factory act. And industrial unit comes under the factory act if it employees 10 workers or more with the use of electric power. While all such measures intending to give benefits to a worker should be welcomed, sometimes these measures become a burden for an employer because of the poor performance of his enterprise or misuse of these measures by workers. An attempt was, therefore, made to see whether the sample entrepreneurs considered the labour laws as problem, and if so, what was the relative importance of the individual measures.

Only about one fourth of the sample entrepreneurs felt that the labour laws were problems. The ESI was found to be the most difficult problem for the sample entrepreneurs in the initial year. This was followed by the provision of factory act, minimum salary/wage and minimum bonus (Table 6.8).

During the period 1985-88, the provision for minimum wage/salary was found to be the most difficult problem, followed by the ESI, factory act, provident funds and minimum bonus (Table 6.8).

TABLE 6.8: Relative Importance of the Nature of Labour-Law Problems faced by Sample Units in the Initial Year and the Period 1985-88 by Performance-Group

Nature of Labour Law Problem	VSU		SU		AVU		SIKU		Total	
	1*	2*	1	2	1	2	1	2	1	2
Factory Act	3	1	3	2	1	4	—	5	2	3
Minimum Wage/Salary	2	4	4	1	2	1	—	1	2	1
Perks	4	5	5	6	5	6	—	5	5	6
Minimum Bonus	5	6	1	5	2	5	—	4	4	5
Provident Fund	5	3	5	4	4	3	—	3	6	6
Employees State Insurance (ESI)	1	2	1	3	5	2	—	2	1	2

* 1 — Initial Year; 2 — 1985-88

The main problem on account of factory act faced by some of the entrepreneurs was that once they came under the factory act, they had to extend all the welfare measures to their workers even when performance of their enterprises was not upto the mark or even when they were sick. Such entrepreneurs, therefore, tried their best to remain outside the factory act, even by resorting to some malpractices. The main problem faced by the entrepreneurs, with regard to ESI, was its misuse by workers. Many of the sample entrepreneurs complained that workers often obtained false medical certificates and took advantage of the ESI facility on that basis while they were actually working for somebody else during the period of their so-called illness or other health problems. The sample entrepreneurs were generally not against giving bonus to their workers but they felt that it should be linked with their performance instead of being mandatory. The same plea was made by them with regard to the minimum salary or wage.

Management Problem

Most of the sample entrepreneurs did not seem to have made any critical assessment of their own functioning as entrepreneur-managers and that of their enterprises. Even if some of them had some idea of shortcomings in the management of their enterprises, they were shy to reveal the same because they might have felt that any shortcoming in the management of their enterprises would have reflection on their own functioning. Such inhibitions are natural when there is no distinction between the organisational achievements or failures and the achievements or failures of any entrepreneur-manager. However, such inhibitions on the part of an entrepreneur-manager are indications of the lack of professional approach to the management of his or her enterprise. Only about 14 per cent of the sample entrepreneurs came forward to furnish information on the management problems of their enterprises.

On the bias of information furnished by the sample entrepreneurs, problem in the production management was found to be the most difficult one in the initial year. This was followed by the problems in financial management, labour management, marketing management, information management, communication management, and organisational management (Table 6.9).

TABLE 6.9: Relative Importance of the Nature of Management Problem faced by Sample Units in the Initial Year by Performance-Group

Nature of Management Problem	VSU		SU		AVU		SIKU		Total	
	1*	2*	1	2	1	2	1	2	1	2
Production Management	1	3	1	1	1	3	1	—	1	1
Financial Management	4	4	2	3	2	1	—	—	2	2
Labour Management	3	2	3	2	2	2	3	—	3	4
Marketing Management	1	1	7	5	7	6	1	1	4	3
Information Management	6	6	5	7	6	4	—	—	5	6
Communication Management	7	6	4	4	4	5	—	—	6	7
Organisational Management	5	4	5	6	4	—	—	—	7	5

* 1 — Initial; 2 — 1985-88

During the period 1985-88, production management and financial management continued to be the first and second most difficult problem-areas as in the initial years. Marketing management was found to be third most difficult problem-area during this period followed by labour management, organisational management, information management, and communication management. There were some changes in the relative importance of management problem-areas during the period 1985-88 over that in the initial year. While the problems of marketing management and organisational management had become relatively more important, the relative importance of labour management, information management and communication management had gone down. In the sick group, only marketing management was indicated to be the problem-area (Table 6.9).

Government Policies and Rules

The government policies and rules also affect the functioning of a SSI unit by imposing certain restrictions or levying additional taxes. Sometimes, a very complicated procedure and the required detailed documentation of information lead to additional financial burden on an entrepreneur. Also, too many rules and regulations sometimes become handy for some of the government officials to harass an entrepreneur with genuine problems. All these affect the functioning of an enterprise and the decision-making process of an entrepreneur. An attempt was, therefore, made to study as to how many of the sample entrepreneurs felt that some of the government policies and rules (apart from the labour laws) created problems for them and what was their relative importance. About one-third of sample entrepreneurs felt that different government policies and rules affected their units to a varying degree.

Among the individual government policies and rules, the provision of sales tax was found to be the most problematic one in the initial year. This was followed by the provisions of excise duty, income tax, and export-import policy. Sales-tax was found to be the most problematic in all the performance-groups except the average group in the initial year. In the average group, the provision of excise duty was found to be the most problematic (Table 6.10). During the period 1985-88, the provision of excise duty was found to be the most problematic, followed by the provisions of sales tax, income tax and export-import policy.

TABLE 6.10: Relative Importance of the Government Policies and Rules causing problem in the Initial Year and the Period 1985-88 by Performance-Group

Nature of GPR Problem	VSU		SU		AVU		SIKU		Total	
	1*	2*	1	2	1	2	1	2	1	2
Excise Duty	—	1	2	2	1	1	—	2	2	1
Income Tax	3	3	3	3	3	3	—	4	3	3
Sales Tax	1	2	1	1	2	2	1	1	1	2
Export-Import Policy	—	—	4	4	—	—	—	3	4	4

* 1 — Initial Year; 2 — 1985-88

The entrepreneurs, who felt that the excise duty was a problem for them, revealed that the main problem was not the rate of excise duty but the complicated procedure involved and the required detailed documentation. Even a minor mistake in the procedure or documentation became a source of harassment by the concerned officials. A small entrepreneur, whose turnover was not substantially greater than the excise limit of Rs. 1,500,000, therefore, generally tried to understate the size of annual turnover of his enterprise in order to avoid his enterprise coming under the net of excise duty. Only when his turnover went well beyond the excise limit and he was sure of at least maintaining that level of turnover that he declared the size of turnover being greater than the excise limit. The excise duty was reported to have restrained the growth of turnover to a certain extent.

With regard to the sales tax too, the entrepreneurs were not so much concerned about the rates of sales tax as the procedure involved and other problems. They felt that the collection of sales tax and the maintenance of information took a lot of their time. Sometimes, sales tax affected the sale of their products in other states as well as in Karnataka if the sales tax had been exempted on that product or the rate of sales tax was lower in other states. Some of the entrepreneurs opined that there should be uniform rates of sales taxes all over the country.

Other Problems

A few entrepreneurs felt that some of the statutory obligations were problem for them. On the basis of very limited information available, it was found that getting licenses was the most difficult problem. This was followed by the obligation to submit annual returns, complying with the standing orders of government, and the measures of pollution control, etc. A few of the sample entrepreneurs felt that they faced some problems with regard to technical and consultancy services. The high cost of technical and consultancy services was found to be the most difficult problem, followed by its non-availability, ineffectiveness, and untimely availability.

Serious Problems and Efforts to Overcome

It is often said that a SSI enterprise is very vulnerable during its initial stage and with age it acquires a greater strength to withstand the adverse impact of external factors as well as internal factors. An attempt was, therefore, made to study the serious problems faced by the sample SSI units, at the different stages, that might have left some lasting impact on the units. Also, information on the efforts made by the sample entrepreneurs in order to overcome the individual problems, and the effectiveness of each effort were obtained. The problems faced in different years by the sample units were grouped into three:

(i) problems faced during the first year to the fourth year;
(ii) problems faced during the fifth year to the ninth year; and
(iii) problems faced after the ninth year, since establishment.

About 16 per cent of the sample units had faced marketing problems, 14 per cent financial problems, 5 per cent production problems, and 4 per cent labour problems during the first year to the fourth year since their establishments. During the period of fifth year to the ninth year, 6 per cent of the sample units had faced serious financial problems, 7 per cent had faced labour problems, and about 8 per cent had faced marketing problems. During the period of after 9th year of their establishments, 13 per cent of the units had faced serious marketing problems, 7 per cent had faced financial problems, 4 per cent labour problems, and 3 per cent production problems.

An analysis of these problems faced during the three periods revealed that the units belonging to the very successful group and successful group too had faced similar problems as faced by the units belonging to the average group and sick group. In fact the proportion of such units was rather greater in the very successful group and successful group. As such, the outstanding performance of very successful group and reasonably good performance of the units belonging to successful group could neither be because of the lack of problems nor the poor or unsatisfactory performance of the units belonging to the average group and sick group could be attributed to the serious problems faced by them.

The entrepreneurs, whose units had faced different serious problems during the three periods discussed above, had made different efforts for overcoming the problems. Out of 40 efforts to overcome the financial problems, only 18 per cent could succeed fully, 47 per cent could succeed partly, and the remaining 35 per cent could not succeed at all. Out of 17 efforts made to overcome the serious production problems, 59 per cent had succeeded fully, 23 per cent had succeeded partly, and 18 per cent did not succeed at all. Out of 24 efforts made to overcome the labour problems, about 46 per cent had been fully successful, 50 per cent had been partly successful, and 4 per cent did not succeed at all. Out of 47 efforts made to overcome the marketing problems, 32 per cent had been fully successful, 51 per cent partly successful, and the remaining 17 per cent did not succeed at all.

From the preceding discussion it is obvious that the entrepreneurs found it relatively easier to overcome the production problems and labour problems than marketing problems and financial problems. The overcoming of financial problems appeared to the most difficult one.

Summary

In the initial year, the extent of availability of required inputs, facilities, and demand for product for the sample as a whole was worked out to be over 90 per cent. A comparison of the extent of availability across the performance-groups revealed that the extent of availability in the initial year was greater in the average group and sick group than that in the very successful group and successful group. As such, the units belonging to the average group and sick group did not have any major disadvantage in comparison to those belonging to the very successful group and successful group at the initial stage. However, the availability of working capital and demand for products had declined significantly, during the period 1985-88, in the case of sick group.

Among the major operational problems faced by the sample units in the initial year, the marketing problems were found to be the most difficult ones, followed by the shortage of working capital, labour problem, inadequacy of capital for fixed investment, power supply problem, and so on. During the period 1985-88, shortage of working capital was found to be the most difficult problem, followed by labour problem, marketing problem, power supply problem, and so on. Though the relative importance of individual operational problems varied significantly across the performance-groups, no definite pattern was found either in the initial year or during the period 1985-88.

As per the nature of operational problems, high cost and scarcity were the major problems with regard to raw materials. Inadequacy and uncertainty were the major problems with regard to power supply. Demand on credit and competition from other SSI units were the major marketing problems. Lack of skilled workers, absenteeism, and job-hopping were found to be the major labour problems. As per the problems on account of labour laws, the provisions of ESI and minimum wage/salary were reported to be the most vexing ones. The main complaint against the ESI was its misuse by workers. The major management problem-areas identified were production, finance, marketing and labour. Among the government policies and rules, the provisions of excise duty and sales tax were identified as the major problem areas. The entrepreneurs were not so much concerned about the rates of excise duties and sales tax as about the procedure and detailed documentations involved.

An analysis of the nature of serious problems faced by the sample units in all the four performance-groups at three stages (during the first four years, fifth year to ninth year, and after ninth year) revealed that some of the units belonging to all the four groups had faced similar problems at all the three stages. As such, the better performance of very successful group and successful group could not be due to the lack of serious problems. The analysis of efforts made by the entrepreneurs to overcome the serious problems forced by them revealed that it was easier to overcome the production problems and labour problems than the financial problems and marketing problems.

7

PERFORMANCE AND RESPONSIBLE FACTOR

PERFORMANCE

The performance of sample SSI units belonging to the four groups is discussed in terms of:

- annual growth (compound) of capital for fixed investment, working capital, total productive capital, turnover and employment;
- annual growth (compound) of per employee fixed capital, working capital, total productive capital, and turnover;
- ratio of working capital to capital for fixed investment, ratio of turnover to fixed capital, working capital, and total productive capital; and
- outstanding capital borrowed for fixed investment in relation to the net increase in the borrowed capital for fixed investment.

Annual Growth of Capital and Turnover

Fixed Capital

The average annual growth rate of capital for fixed investment* for the sample as a whole was found to be 9 per cent. It ranged between 23 per cent in the case of very successful group and 3 per cent in the case of

* In this study, capital for fixed investment refers to the fixed investment on plant and machinery only.

average group. The growth rate being about 6 per cent in the case of sick group was almost double of that in the case of average group. In the case of successful group, the growth rate was slightly above the average growth rate (Table 7.1).

Working Capital

The average annual growth rate of working capital for the sample as a whole was found to be about 12 per cent. It was the greatest in the very successful group (25%), followed by the successful group (16%), and average group (8%). The sick group had witnessed a negative growth rate of one per cent (Table 7.1).

Total Productive Capital

The total productive capital for the sample as a whole had grown at the rate 10 per cent. It was found to be the greatest in the very successful group (24%), followed by the successful group (11%), average group (5%), and sick group (2%). Thus, the growth rate of total productive capital was greater in the better performing group (Table 7.1).

Turnover

The average annual growth rate of turnover for the sample as a whole was found to be 19 per cent. It was the greatest in the very successful group (33%), followed by the successful group (23%), average group (9%) and sick group (3%). Thus, the growth rate of turnover also was found to be greater in the better performing group (Table 7.1).

Employment

The employment, for the sample as a whole, had grown at the rate of 7 per cent. It was found to be the greatest in the very successful group (13%), followed by the successful group (10%), average group (4%), and sick group (2%). Thus, the growth rate of employment across the performance-groups had followed the same pattern as the growth rates of total productive capital and turnover (Table 7.1).

The growth rates discussed above indicated that the performance of very successful group had been outstanding with regard to all the five indices, i.e., the growth rates of fixed capital, working capital, total productive capital, turnover and employment. The performance of successful group was though well below the performance-level of very successful group in respect of all the five indices, it was much above the performance of average group and sick group. Further the growth rates in the case of successful group were greater than the average growth rates in respect of all the five indices. On the other hand, the growth rates with regards to all the five indices in the average group and sick group were well below the average growth rates for the sample as a whole. The performance of average group was better than that of sick group with regard to all but one indicator (i.e., growth of fixed capital).

TABLE 7.1: Compound Annual Growth Rate (in %) of Capital, Turnover and Employment by Performance-Group

Item	VSU	SU	AVU	SIKU	Total
Fixed Capital	22.7	9.4	3.3	5.8	9.2
Working Capital	25.1	16.2	7.7	–1.0	11.7
Total Productive Capital (Fixed + Working)	23.8	11.4	4.7	2.2	10.1
Turnover	37.6	22.8	9.2	3.3	19.1
Employment	13.2	9.7	4.4	1.7	7.3

Capital and Turnover Per Employee

Fixed Capital

The fixed capital per employee for all the sample units in the initial year was worked out to be Rs. 28,800 and it had gone up to Rs. 34,700 in the year 1987-88, recording an increase of about 21 per cent. In the initial year, the fixed capital per employee was found to be the largest in the successful group (Rs. 46,100), followed by the average group (Rs. 32,000), sick group (Rs. 17,400), and very successful group (Rs. 15,800). In the year 1987-88, it ranged between Rs. 26,900 in the case of sick group and Rs. 44,700 in the case of successful group. While the fixed capital per employee in the year 1987-88 over that in the initial year had increased by 105 per cent in the case of very successful group and by 55 per cent in the case of sick group, the same had declined by 3 per cent in the successful group and by 9 per cent in the case of average group (Table 7.2). Though fixed capital per employee had declined by 3 per cent in the successful group, yet it was the highest (Rs. 44,700) among all the performance-groups. The decline in the successful group was due to the higher growth rate of employment which was 10 per cent against the 9 per cent growth rate of fixed capital. The same was true in the case of average group where employment had grown at the rate of 4.4 per cent while the fixed capital had grown at the rate of 3.3 per cent only. On the other hand, while employment had grown at the rate of only 2 per cent in the sick group, the fixed capital had grown at the rate of about 6 per cent.

The average annual growth rate (compound) was worked out to be 2 per cent. It was found to be the greatest in the very successful group (8%) followed by the sick group (4%). The successful group and average group had witnessed negative growth rates of 0.3 per cent and 0.9 per cent respectively.

Working Capital

The working capital per employee for all the sample units in the initial year was found to be Rs. 15,400 and it had gone upto Rs. 23,400 by the year 1987-88, recording an increase of 52 per cent. The working capital per employee in the initial year ranged between Rs. 11,700 in the case of average group and Rs. 26,600 in the case of sick group. In the year 1987-88, the same was found to be the largest in the case of very successful group (Rs. 28,200), followed by the successful group (Rs. 25,600), sick group (Rs. 19,800), and the average group (Rs. 16,500). The increase in working capital per employee in the year 1987-88 over that of the initial year ranged between 42 per cent in the case of average group and 137 per cent in the case of very successful group. In the case of sick group, it had declined by 26 per cent (Table 7.2). Though the increase in the case of average group was about 42 per cent, the per employee working capital continued to be the smallest among the four groups.

The average annual growth rate (compound) of working capital per employee was worked out to be 4 per cent for the total sample. It was found to be the greatest in the very successful group (10%), followed by the successful group (6%), and average group (3%). The sick group had witnessed a negative growth rate of 3 per cent.

Total Productive Capital

The total productive capital per employee for all the sample units was worked out to be Rs. 44,200 in the initial year and it had gone upto Rs. 58,100 in the year 1987-88, recording an increase of 31 per cent. The total productive capital per employee was the largest in the successful group (Rs. 60,000), followed by the average group (Rs. 44,400), sick group (Rs. 44,000) and the very successful group (Rs. 27,800) in the initial year. In the year 1987-88, it ranged between Rs, 45,600 in the case of average group and Rs. 70,300 in the case of successful group. The very successful group had experienced the highest growth of about 118 per cent, and the average group had experienced the lowest growth of 3 per cent in the year 1987-88 over that in the initial year. Even in the case of successful group, the growth being 17 per cent was rather modest (Table 7.2).

TABLE 7.2: Capital and Annual Turnover Per Employee in the Initial Year and the Year 1987-88

Per Employee Capital and Turnover (Rs. in 000)	VSU	SU	AVU	SIKU	Total
Fixed Capital					
Initial Year	15.8	46.1	32.0	17.4	28.8
1987-88	32.4	44.7	29.0	26.9	34.7
Percentage Change	205.1	97.0	90.6	154.6	120.5
Working Capital					
Initial Year	11.9	13.9	11.7	26.6	15.4
1987-88	28.2	25.6	16.6	19.8	23.4
Percentage Change	237.0	184.2	141.9	74.4	152.0
Total Productive Capital					
Initial Year	27.8	60.0	44.4	44.0	44.2
1987-88	60.5	70.3	45.6	46.7	58.1
Percentage Change	217.6	117.2	102.7	106.1	131.4
Annual Turnover					
Initial Year	20.9	26.0	34.2	29.4	28.2
1987-88	126.7	85.7	56.1	34.9	84.9
Percentage Change	606.2	329.6	164.0	118.7	301.1

The average annual growth rate (compound) of total productive capital per employee was worked out to be 3 per cent for all the sample units. It was found to be the greatest in the very successful group (9%), followed by the successful group (1.5%), sick group (0.5%) and average group (0.2%).

As a whole, the analysis of per employee capital in the initial year and the year 1987-88 revealed that though the per employee capital base in the initial year was quite strong in the case of successful group, average group, and sick group, the growth of per employee capital had not been impressive. On the other hand, even though the per employee capital base was the weakest in the case of very successful group, its growth had been very impressive.

Annual Turnover

The annual turnover per employee for all the sample units was worked out to be Rs. 28,200 in the initial year and it had gone up to Rs. 84,900 by the year 1987-88, recording an increase of 201 per cent. The per employee annual turnover in the initial year was found to be the smallest in the case of very successful group (Rs. 20,900) and the largest in the case of average group (Rs. 34,200). In the year 1987-88, the smallest annual turnover per employee was found in the case of sick group (Rs. 34,900) and the largest in the very successful group (Rs. 126,700). While growth per employee in annual turnover for the year 1987-88 over that of the initial year was more than five folds (506%) in the case of very successful group, and 230 per cent in the case of successful group, it was only 64 per cent in the average group and merely 19 per cent in the case of sick group (Table 7.2).

The average annual growth rate (compound) of annual turnover per employee for all the sample units was worked out to be 11 per cent. It was found to the greatest in the very successful group (21%) followed by the successful group (12%), average group (5%) and sick group (2%).

On the basis of the foregoing analysis of the growth rates of capital and turnover per employee, it is clear that the performance of very successful group was outstanding with regard to growth in capital per employee as well as per employee turnover. In the case of successful group, though the growth rate in capital per employee was not significant, the growth rate in turnover per employee was quite impressive. On the other hand, the performance of average group was insignificant with regard to the growth in capital per employee and modest with regard to the growth of turnover per employee. As for the sick group, its performance was low with regard to the growth in capital per employee as well as turnover per employee.

One of the assumptions with regard to the policy support in the favour of SSI sector has been that a SSI unit can generate greater employment with relatively smaller capital investment. If this assumption is accepted in a simple way, a gradual reduction in capital per employee in a SSI unit would be an indicator of the efficiency of a unit. However, such a situation can hardly be expected in an era of technological boom and competition, when there is so much stress on the modernisation of technology. In such a situation, there is bound to be greater capital investment per employee, particularly if a SSI unit is expected to grow. The important point, in such a situation, would be not the smaller size of capital investment per employee but the efficient utilization of capital invested per employee. Therefore, the ratio of turnover per employee to capital per employee at two (at least) different points of time or periods would indicate whether there has been improvement or deterioration — in the utilization of capital as well as manpower. With this in view, the ratios of turnover per employee to total productive capital per employee were calculated for the initial year and the year 1987-88.

The ratio for the sample as a whole was found to be 0.6 in the initial year and 1.5 in the year 1987-88. Thus, the utilization efficiency had improved by about 150 per cent. In the initial year, the ratio was found to be the highest in the very successful group and average group (0.8), followed by the sick group (0.7), and successful group (0.4). In the year 1987-88, it was the highest in the very successful group (2.1), followed by the successful and average groups (1.2), and sick group (0.8). Thus, the utilization in the year 1987-88 was the most efficient in the very successful group and least efficient in the sick group. The improvement in the utilization was found to be the greatest in the successful group and smallest in the sick group. However, the efficiency level in the successful group despite maximum improvement (200%), was at the same level as that of the average group in the year 1987-88 because the efficiency level was very low in the initial year in the successful group.

Financial Ratios

Ratio of Working Capital to Fixed Capital

The ratio of working capital to fixed capital (RWF) for all the sample units in the initial year was found to be 0.5.

- It was found to be maximum in the sick group (1.5), followed by
- very successful group (0.8);
- average group (0.4); and
- successful group (0.3).

By the year 1987-88, the average RWF for all the sample units had gone upto 0.7, recording an increase of 40 per cent. Among the four performance groups, while the successful group had experienced maximum growth of 100 per cent and average group 50 per cent in the RWF, the RWF had declined by 53 per cent in the sick group in 1987-88 over that in the initial year. The RWF had increased by only 13 per cent in the case of very successful group. However, the RWF in the very successful group was quite high (0.8) in the initial year itself, and though it had increased by only 13 per cent by the year 1987-88 over that in the initial year, it was found to be the highest (0.9) among all the four performance groups in the year 1987-88. On the other hand, the RWFs in the case of successful group and average group were only 0.6 in the year 1987-88 despite a steep increase of about 100 per cent and 50 per cent respectively--because their RWF was rather low in the initial year (Table 7.3). From the RWF across the performance-groups, it is obvious that the financial structure in the case of very successful group was better balanced since the beginning in comparison to the same in other performance-groups. Even though the growth in the very successful group had been very impressive with regard to the fixed investment, turnover and employment, there had not been any significant change in the composition of capital.

Ratio of Turnover to Fixed Capital

The ratio of turnover to fixed capital (RTF) for all the sample units in the initial year was found to be 1.0. Among the performance-groups, the RTF ranged between 0.5 in the case of successful group and 1.6 in the case of sick group in the initial year. By the year 1987-88, the RTF for all the sample units had gone up to 2.5, recording an increase of about 150 per cent. A comparison of RTF across the performance-groups in the year 1987-88, revealed that it was the largest in the case of very successful group (4.5) and smallest in the case of sick group (1.3). The growth of RTF in the year 1987-88 over that in the initial year ranged between about 73 per cent in the case of average group and about 280 per cent in the case of successful group. In the sick group, it had declined by 19 per cent (Table 7.3).

Thus, there had been improvement in the efficient utilization of fixed capital as the RTF had increased by 150 per cent. Among the performance-groups, the utilization of fixed capital was the most efficient in the very successful group and least efficient in the sick group. In the successful and average groups, the efficiency of the utilization of fixed capital was at the same level.

TABLE 7.3: Ratios in the Initial Year and the Year 1987-88

Ratio	VSU	SU	AVU	SIKU	Total
Ratio of Working Capital to Fixed Capital:					
Initial Year	0.8	0.3	0.4	1.5	0.5
1987-88	0.9	0.6	0.6	0.7	0.7
Ratio of Turnover to Fixed Capital:					
Initial Year	1.4	0.5	1.1	1.6	1.0
1987-88	4.5	1.9	1.9	1.3	2.5
Ratio of Turnover to Working Capital:					
Initial Year	1.8	1.9	2.9	1.1	1.8
1987-88	3.9	3.4	3.4	1.8	3.6
Ratio of Turnover to Total Productive Capital:					
Initial Year	0.8	0.4	0.8	0.7	0.6
1987-88	2.1	1.2	1.2	0.8	1.5

Ratio of Turnover to Working Capital

In the initial year, the ratio of turnover to working capital (RTW) for all the units was worked out to be 1.8. It ranged between 1.1 in the case of sick group and 2.9 in the case of average group. The RTW for all the sample units had gone up from 1.8 in the initial year to 3.6 in the year 1987-88, recording an increase of 100 per cent. As for the performance-groups, the RTW, in the year 1987-88, ranged between 1.8 in the case of sick group and 3.9 in the case of very successful group. The percentage increase in the RTW in the year 1987-88 over that in the initial year was found to be the greatest in the very successful group (117) followed by the successful group (79), sick group (64), and average group (17) (Table 7.3).

Thus, the utilization of working capital for the sample as a whole had improved by 100 per cent. In the initial year, the utilization of working capital was the most efficient in the average group and the least efficient in the sick group. In the year 1987-88, it was found to be the most efficient in the very successful group, followed by the successful and average groups. The efficiency of utilization was the least in the sick group.

Ratio of Turnover to Total Productive Capital (RTTPC)

The ratio of turnover to total productive capital for all the sample units in the initial year was worked out to be 0.6 and it had gone upto 1.5 by the year 1987-88, recording an increase of about 150 per cent. In the initial year, the RTTPC ranged between 0.4 in the case of successful group and 0.8 in the case of very successful and average groups. The same in the year 1987-88 ranged between 0.8 in the case of sick group and 2.1 in the case of very successful group. The percentage increase of RTTPC in the year 1987-88 over that in the initial year was found to be the greatest in successful group (200), followed by the very successful group (163), average group (50) and sick group (14) (Table 7.3).

Thus, the utilization of total productive capital for the sample as a whole had improved by 150 per cent. The efficiency-level of the utilization of total productive capital, in the initial year, was the maximum in the very successful and average groups and the minimum in the successful group. In 1987-88, the same was found to be the maximum in the very successful group, followed by the successful and average groups, and the sick group.

Outstanding Borrowed Capital for Fixed Investment

Default in the repayment of certain term loan instalments has been indicated by the RBI as one of the criteria for determining the sickness of SSI units. While the details of defaults in the repayment of term loan instalments could not be obtained, it was possible to obtain the outstanding amount of borrowed capital for fixed investment against the sample units at the time of survey. This information was analysed to see the extent of outstanding borrowed capital for fixed investment across the four performance-groups. The outstanding borrowed capital has been analysed in two parts — (1) borrowed capital for fixed investment in the initial year, and (2) the total borrowed capital for fixed investment till 1987-88.

Borrowed Capital for Fixed Investment in the Initial Year

It has already been discussed in Chapter 5 that the average fixed investment in the sample units was Rs. 278,600 in the initial year. The share of borrowed capital for fixed investment to the total fixed investment in the initial year for the total sample units was worked out to be 67 per cent. The share of such borrowed capital was found to be the largest in the sick group (75%), followed by the very successful group (72%), successful group (70%), and average group (65%). The percentage of outstanding capital borrowed for fixed investment in the initial year was found to be 44 per cent for all the sample units. The percentage of outstanding fixed capital to the borrowed fixed capital in the initial year was 3 per cent in the very successful group, 19 per cent in the successful group, 41 per cent in the average group, and 143 per cent in the sick group. Thus, the repayment behaviour of sample entrepreneurs with regard to the capital borrowed for fixed investment in the initial year was found to be the best in the very successful group, followed by the successful group, average group and sick group.

Borrowed Capital for Fixed Investment till the Year 1987-88

The average fixed investment for all the sample units, in the year 1987-88, wa found to be Rs. 633,200. The proportion of borrowed capital for f xed investment to the total fixed investment, till the year 1987-88, was found to be 65 per cent for the total sample. As for the performance-groups, the share of borrowed capital for fixed investment to the total fixed investment ranged between 65 per cent in the case of average group and 76 per cent in the case of sick group. The percentage of total borrowed capital for fixed investment till 1987-88, to the borrowed capital for fixed investment in the initial year for the total sample was worked out to be 240. The same was found to be the greatest in the very successful group (720), followed by the successful group (240), sick group (160) and average group (140). Thus, the net increase in the borrowed capital for fixed investment over the initial borrowed capital was 620 per cent in the very successful group, 140 per cent in the successful group, 40 per cent in the average group, and 60 per cent in the sick group. Against this, the total outstanding borrowed capital for fixed investment, in the year 1987-88, was 27 per cent in the case of very successful group, 23 per cent in the case of successful group, 39 per cent in the case of average group, and 137 per cent in the case of sick group.

Thus, the repayment behaviour of very successful entrepreneurs was the best as in spite of the six fold net increase in the borrowed capital for fixed investment till 1987-88, the outstanding borrowed capital was only 27 per cent. On the other hand, while the net increase in the borrowed capital for fixed investment was only 40 per cent in the average group and 60 per cent in the sick group, the outstanding borrowed capital was 39 per cent and 137 per cent respectively. The outstanding amount in the case of sick group being 137 per cent indicated tha the repayment of borrowed loan was so poor that the outstanding amount had become greater than the principal amount borrowed.

RESPONSIBLE FACTORS FOR PERFORMANCE

Each of the sample entrepreneurs was asked to indicate a set of factors responsible for the performance of his enterprise and to rank each factor in order of its importance, i.e., in order of the impact of individual factors on the performance of unit — giving first rank to the factor having the greatest impact, second rank to the next important factor, and so on. On the basis of this information, the Weighted Rank Index of each factor was worked out in order to determine its relative importance.

The Very Successful and Successful groups

In the very successful group:

- the ability and environment of the entrepreneur was found to be the most important factor; followed by sustaining and improving the quality of products and maintaining production schedules;
- good relationship with the customers and suppliers; good demand for product and proper marketing strategies; adequate and timely supports from the financing banks; good labour

relations;
- proper planning and effective management of units; and
- ancillary relationship with large firms.

Thus, eight responsible factors, in order of their importance, were identified for the outstanding performance of the units belonging to the very successful group (Table 7.4).

In the successful group too, the ability and environment of the entrepreneur was found to be the most important factor responsible for the performance of sample units. This was followed by:

- good demand for products and proper marketing strategies;
- sustaining and improving the quality of products; and maintaining production schedules;
- proper planning and effective management;
- adequate and timely supports from the financing bank;
- good labour relations;
- ancillary relationship with large firms; and
- good relationship with customers and suppliers (Table 7.4).

While there was a good deal of similarity between the very successful group and successful group with regard to the relative importance of factors responsible for the performance of respective groups, there were some significant differences as well. The very successful entrepreneurs seemed to be attaching greater importance to sustaining and improving the quality of their products and maintaining production schedules while the successful entrepreneurs seemed to have greater dependence on demand for their products and marketing strategies adopted by them. Similarly, while the very successful entrepreneurs appeared to be attaching a lot of importance to maintaining good relationships with their customers and suppliers, the successful entrepreneurs did not seem to give that much importance to this factor.

In order to facilitate a better understanding, individual factors responsible for the performance of two groups of sample units are explained hereunder. These explanations are based on the details given by the sample entrepreneurs in the course of identifying the responsible factors.

Ability and Environment of Entrepreneur

Most of the entrepreneurs belonging to the two groups stressed that their capacity and willingness to work hard and keep patience even in the most trying circumstances had contributed a lot to the success of their units. Also, their courage to take up challenges on the basis of their knowledge, training and experience had helped their units in coming out of woods on certain occasions. Another personality attribute of these entrepreneurs was reported to be honesty in business (i.e., being honest to oneself). According to them, their being honest to themselves had motivated them to make a proper assessment of their business environment and the management of their enterprises, identify strengths and weaknesses of the management of their enterprises in the given business environment, adopt measures required to overcome the weaknesses of management, and adapt themselves to the existing as well as changing features of their business environment. Their immediate social environment, i.e., the health and happiness of the members of their families and the encouragement and cooperation received from the family members, particularly when required most, had contributed a lot to their ability and preparedness to overcome the problems and take-up new challenges. In the case of partnership concerns, mutual understanding, trust and confidence among the partners were reported to be one of the most vital factors for the success of such enterprises.

TABLE 7.4: Relative Importance of Factors Responsible for the Performance of Sample Units belonging to the Very Successful Group (VSU) and Successful Group (SU)

Responsible Factor	VSU	SU
Ability and Environment of Entrepreneur	1	1
Sustaining and Improving Product Quality and Maintaining Production Schedules	2	3
Good Relationship with customers and suppliers	3	8
Good demand for products and proper Marketing Strategies	4	2
Adequate and Timely Supports from Bank	5	5
Good Labour Relations	6	6
Proper planning and effective management	6	4
Ancillary relationship with large frims	7	7

Sustaining and Improving Product Quality and Maintaining

Production Schedules: The sample entrepreneurs belonging to the two groups emphasised that not only they tried their best to sustain the quality of their products but also continued their efforts to identify the need and find ways and means for improving the quality of their products. At the same time, they tried to diversify their product-range and activities in order to overcome the problems of limited demand, and thereby maximise the utilization of their units' production capacities. Further, it was reported that they were generally able to maintain their production schedules by motivating workers, ensuring adequate and timely supply of the required raw materials and other essential inputs, and proper maintenance of plants and machineries.

Maintaining Good Relationship with Customers and Suppliers

According to the sample entrepreneurs, maintaining good relationship with customers involved delivery of goods on schedule, provision of service after sales, and ensuring overall satisfaction of customers by maintaining good quality of products and attending to their complaints. The maintaining of good relationship with suppliers involved payment to them on time.

Good Demand for Products and Proper Marketing Strategy

The sample entrepreneurs belonging to both the very successful group and successful group revealed that though there was a good demand for their products, they were well aware of the dangerous implications of being dependent on sole or a few buyers/or a single product. They were, therefore, trying their best to keep their product-range and markets as diversified as possible within the given limits. Also, they tried to make their products attractive by offering them on a competitive price. Even with a good quality of products and competitive price, continued efforts to retain the existing buyers and find out new ones were reported to be the essential conditions for the success of their units.

Adequate and Timely Support from Financing Banks

Though the sample entrepreneurs belonging to both the groups faced inadequacy of working capital, they did not find much problem in dealing with their banks and financial institutions. They observed that their banks generally came forward to providing additional financial support as and when required. They felt that the success of their units could be attributed to a certain extent to the timely financial support provided by their banks.

Good Labour Relations

A majority of sample entrepreneurs belonging to both successful and very successful groups observed that their units were generally free of labour problems. Over the years, they had developed mutual confidence with a majority of their employees who identified themselves with the units. Also, they tried their best to keep their employees happy by giving some incentives and perquisites from time to time. Though there might have been some minor problems now and then, generally good labour relations prevailed in their units.

Proper Planning and Management

A number of the sample entrepreneurs observed that the application of scientific methods to the overall planning and management of units; proper material management; financial planning and discipline; demand forecasting; and taking right decisions at the right time were some of the aspects of planning and management that had contributed to the success of their units.

The Average and Sick Groups

In the average group, the performance of sample units was attributed to a combination of favourable factors and unfavourable factors. Sustaining and improving product quality was found to be the most important factor, followed by the demand for product and marketing strategies adopted by the entrepreneurs. The third most important factors were stiff competition, delayed payment and other marketing problems. The ability of entrepreneur, and good relationship with customers and suppliers were found to be the fourth and fifth most important factors. Other factors identified in order of importance, were planning and management, good labour relations, shortage of working capital, ancillary relationship with large firms, illness (self and in family) and conflict among partners (Table 7.5). Thus, the entrepreneurs belonging to the average group seemed to have greater dependence on the quality of their products and demand for the same than on their own entrepreneurial abilities to intervene into the environment in order to carve out a niche for them.

TABLE 7.5: Relative Importance of Factors Responsible for the Performance of Sample Units belonging to the Average Group

Responsible Factor	Rank
Sustaining and Improving Product Quality	1
Demand for Product and Marketing Strategies	2
Stiff Competition, Delayed payment and other Marketing Problems*	3
Ability of Entrepreneur	4
Good Relationship with Customers and Suppliers	5
Planning and Management	6
Good Labour Relations	7
Shortage of Working Capital*	8
Ancillary Relationship with Large Firms	9
Illness and Conflict*	10

* Unfavourable Factor.

In the sick group, the reported shortage of working capital and non-cooperation from the financing banks were found to be the most important factor. According to the sample entrepreneurs, the shortage of working capital was caused by inadequate sanction of credit limit and in some cases withdrawal of working capital facility by banks, delayed payment and non-realisation of bills, non-lifting of goods (manufactured on orders) by customers, bulk rejection of goods blocking substantial portion of working capital, and diversion of working capital funds for fixed investment and non-productive purposes. The second most important factor was found to be the marketing problems, like stiff competition, undue delay in the realisation of bills, low or lack of demand for products and dependence on a single buyer. The third most important factor was inadequate and untimely support from government agencies, i.e., undue delay in providing required infrastructural facilities that delayed the commencement of production, and non-delivery of promised incentives. The fourth most impo:tant factor was found to be the production problems comprising inadequacy of raw materials, inability to adhere to production-schedules which caused untimely delivery of goods to customers, inability to change product-lines, low-quality of products, high costs of production, and lack of scope for diversifying product-range. Other factors to which the poor performance of sick units was attributed to were obsolescence and non-availability of technology, inexperience of entrepreneur and inefficient management of unit, and labour problems (Table 7.6).

TABLE 7.6: Relative Importance of Factors Responsible for the Performance of Sick Group

Responsible Factor	Rank
Shortage of Working Capital and Non-Co-operation from Bank	1
Stiff Competition, Low Demand, Delayed Payment and other Marketing Problems	2
Inadequate and Untimely Support from Government Agencies	3
Production Problems	4
Obsolescence and Non-availability of Technology	5
Inexperience and Inefficient Management	5
Labour Problem	6

WILLINGNESS FOR MEDIUM SCALE UNIT AND FUTURE PLANS

Willingness for Medium Scale Unit

About 28 per cent of entrepreneurs were willing to allow their units to grow to become medium scale units and the remaining 72 per cent were against it. The proportion of entrepreneurs who wanted their units to grow to become medium scale units was 44 per cent in the very successful group, 36 per cent in the successful group, 24 per cent in the average group and 14 per cent in the sick group. Thus, the proportion of entrepreneurs favouring their units to grow to become medium scale units was greater in the better performing groups.

All the sample entrepreneurs who were in favour of the growth of their units to the level of medium scale units were asked to indicate the advantages of a medium scale unit. On the basis of these entrepreneurs' responses, it was found that the greatest advantage that these entrepreneurs foresaw were that it would be possible to reduce cost of production; and expansion, diversification and modernisation of their unit would be easier. The percentage frequency of these advantages ranged between 14 in the case of sick group and 50 in the case of average group. The second most important advantage was found to be the reduction in marketing costs and diversification of market. The percentage frequency of this was about 29 in the case of sick group and 20 in other three groups. Other advantages, like greater bargaining power, greater export possibilities, benefits (saving) on tax, taping the already available market, and possibility of fulfilment of desire for growth, etc., were found to be the third set of major advantages. The fourth major advantage was found to be the scope of greater employment opportunities and labour productivity. Other advantages, as foreseen by the entrepreneurs, were that their capacity to raise funds would increase and there would be a diffusion of risks. Also, that there would be a greater possibility for delegation of authority and responsibilities (Table 7.7).

TABLE 7.7: Percentage Frequency of Advantages of a Medium Scale Unit

Advantage	VSU	SU	AVU	SIKU	Total
Reduction in Production Cost, Expansion, Diversification & Modernisation	25.0	30.0	50.0	14.3	32.8
Reduction in Marketing Cost and Diversification of Market	20.0	20.0	20.0	28.6	20.9
Scope for Greater Employment Opportunity and Labour Productivity	10.0	10.0	15.0	14.3	11.9
Increased Fund Raising Capacity and Diffusion of Risk	15.0	10.0	0.0	28.6	10.4
Delegation of Authority/ Responsibility	5.0	15.0	0.0	0.0	6.0
Others	25.0	15.0	15.0	14.3	17.9
Total	100.0	100.0	100.0	100.0	100.0
Total Number	20	20	20	7	67

The major reasons for not intending to become a medium scale entrepreneur was found to be:

- the advantages of remaining a SSI unit (percentage frequency ranged between 21 in the average group and 41 in the sick group);
- unfavourable government policies and complicated procedures;
- the limited managerial capability of entrepreneurs;
- possibility of labour problems because of the large size of employees;

- financial constraints and other problems, like shortage of working space, shortage of electric power, advanced age of entrepreneurs, and lack of motivation on the part of entrepreneur, etc.

Other reasons for not intending to grow to become a medium scale entrepreneue (enterprise) were the possibility of increase in overheaos and thereby, increase in the costs of production, marketing problems, and the problem of infrastructural facilities (Table 7.8).

TABLE 7.8: Percentage Frequency of Reasons for Non-willingness to allow a SSI Unit to grow to become a Medium Scale Unit

Reasons	VSU	SU	AVU	SIKU	Total
Advantages in Remaining Small	33.3	22.4	21.4	41.2	26.1
Possibility of Labour Problem	9.5	12.1	16.7	11.8	13.0
Unfavourable Government Policies and Complicated Procedure	23.8	22.4	7.1	5.9	15.9
Increase in Overheads and Costs of Production	9.5	5.2	7.2	0.0	5.8
Marketing Problems	0.0	1.7	11.9	5.9	5.1
Financial Constraints	4.8	6.9	9.5	11.8	8.0
Limited Managerial Capacity	19.1	15.5	11.9	11.7	14.5
Infrastructure Problem	0.0	6.9	2.4	0.0	3.6
Others	0.0	6.9	11.9	11.7	8.0
Total	100.0	100.0	100.0	100.0	100.0
Total Number	21	58	42	17	138

Future Plans

Out of 120 sample entrepreneurs, 49 entrepreneurs (i.e., 41%) did not have any immediate future plan for their units. Such entrepreneurs accounted for 33 per cent in the very successful group, 52 per cent in the successful group, 47 per cent in the average group, and 14 per cent in the sick group. Thus, the analysis of future plans is based on information furnished by 71 sample entrepreneurs.

Plan for product diversification was found to be the largest one. The percentage frequency of plans for product diversification ranged between 19 per cent in the case of sick group and 54 per cent in the case of average group. The next major plan was for the expansion of existing units, and its percentage frequency ranged between nil in the case of sick group and 29 in the case of successful group. The third major plan was for the expansion and diversification of market, followed by the plan for modernisation of units. In the case of very successful group, the major plan was product diversification, followed by modernisation and expansion of units and expansion and diversification of market. In the case of successful group too, the major plan was product diversification, followed by the expansion of units, modernisation of units and expansion and diversification of market (Table 7.9)

TABLE 7.9: Percentage Frequency of Future Plans of Sample Units by Performance Group

Future Plan	VSU	SU	AVU	SIKU	Total
Modernisation of Unit	22.2	21.4	7.7	7.5	14.1
Expansion of Unit	22.2	28.6	26.9	0.0	19.2
Product Diversification	27.8	32.1	53.9	18.5	33.3
Expansion & Diversification of Market	16.7	17.9	11.5	22.2	17.2
Securing Sub-contract/ Ancillary Relationship	11.1	0.0	0.0	14.8	6.1
Rehabilitation	0.0	0.0	0.0	29.6	8.1
Disposal of Unit	0.0	0.0	0.0	7.4	2.0
Total	100.0	100.0	100.0	100.0	100.0
Total Number	18	28	26	27	99

Thus, there was a great deal of similarity in the future plans of entrepreneurs belonging to the very successful group and the successful group. In the average group, the major plan was for product diversification, followed by expansion of units, expansion and diversification of market, and modernisation of the units. In the sick group, the major plan was found to be the rehabilitation of units. This was followed by the expansion and diversification of market, product diversification and securing sub-contract or ancillary relationship with large firms. While two entrepreneurs belonging to the sick group had plan for the modernisation of their units, two had plan for disposing off their units.

8

SICKNESS AND REHABILITATION

The phenomenal growth of sickness in the SSI sector since the late seventies, the causes of sickness and the official measures for the prevention as well cure of sickness were discussed in Chapter 1. In this chapter, an attempt is being made to analyse the symptoms of sickness, preventive measures taken by the sample entrepreneurs, findings of viability studies, and rehabilitation measures, etc. with regard to the sample sick SSI units.

Out of 120 sample SSI units, 22 units (i.e., 18.3%) were sick. One unit, out of 22 sick units, had become sick within a period of two months after its establishment because of the lack of demand. This unit continued to be sick and there was not much commercial production. In the year 1985, the entrepreneur changed his product from dehyderated green pepper to instant food items. Subsequently, he got good orders for instant food items from the Defence Department. In the meanwhile, he had been pleading with the KSFC to declare his unit sick as he had not been able to repay the term loan instalments. After appraising the projections made by the entrepreneur and the orders he had received from the Defence Department, the KSFC felt, according to the entrepreneur, that his unit could be revived. Accordingly, the KSFC recognised this as a sick unit without declaring it so and rescheduled the repayment of term loan in December 1986. Since then, the units' performance has been improving as its turnover had gone up from Rs. 200,000 in 1985-86 to Rs. 10,00,000 in 1986-87 and come down to Rs. 800,000 in 1987-88. However, because of the past poor performances and mounting liabilities the unit was still in the process of recovery.

Another unit, set up in 1977, became sick at the inception stage itself because of very inadequate working capital, lack of essential raw materials, and undue delay in the commencement of production. After repeated requests by the entrepreneurs, this unit was declared sick by the financing bank in 1982. Without conducting a viability study, the bank simply converted all the overdue loans into term loan, opened a fresh account and enhanced the working capital substantially. However, this unit continued to be sick even at the time of survey in 1988. The annual turnover of the unit had come down from Rs. 650,000 in 1985-86 to Rs. 400,000 in 1986-87, and further to Rs. 300,000 in 1987-88. The ratio of annual turnover to the total operational expenses was worked out to be 1.1 in 1985-86, 0.87 in 1986-87, and 0.76 in 1987-88. The ratio of annual turnover to the total productive capital (fixed capital plus working capital) in 1987-88 was worked out to be 0.40 only.

In the case of another unit, which was sick and had been taken over by a different management, the earlier entrepreneur did not cooperate in giving the details of sickness. Other details of sickness could not be obtained with regard to these three units. Further analysis is, therefore, based on information obtained from the remaining 19 sick units.

Symptoms of Sickness

Out of the 19 units, the symptoms of sickness were noticed in the case of 2 units (10.5%) in the same year in which they were set-up; in 4 units (21%) one year after the establishment; in 7 units (36.8%) between third year and fifth year after the establishment; in 2 units between sixth year and tenth year after establishment, and in the remaining 4 units (21%) after 11 years of establishment. Thus, while the symptoms of sickness were noticed in the case 32 per cent of the units within first three years, in the case of 21 per cent of units it was noticed 11 years after the establishment. This goes to indicate that a SSI unit may become sick at any stage in its life-span.

The entrepreneurs had noticed the symptoms of sickness of their units on their own in the case of 17 units (i.e., 89.5%). In the case of remaining 2 units (10.5%), the symptoms of sickness had been brought to the notice of entrepreneurs by their respective bank branches. Thus, most of the entrepreneurs belonging to the sick group were well aware of the falling health of their units. This may suggest that there is no need for any special measure to monitor the health of SSI units by a third party. What is perhaps needed most is the mutual confidence between an entrepreneur and his financing bank and institution so that there could be mutual exchange of views and facts regarding the health of a SSI unit. Until such a confidence develops, financing banks and institutions have to be extra-vigilant in monitoring the health of financed units on a continuing basis. However, the purpose of such monitoring of the health of assisted units should not be to reprimand the entrepreneurs but to caution them of the danger signals, understand their problems and help them, to the extent possible, in overcoming the problems.

A variety of symptoms of sickness noticed were reported by the 19 entrepreneurs. Out of 50 frequencies of the reported symptoms, mounting liabilities accounted for 42 per cent, shrinking working capital funds for 28 per cent, lack of demand for products for 14 per cent, under utilisation of installed capacity for 12 per cent, and others 4 per cent. Thus, the mounting liabilities and shrinking working capital funds together accounted for 70 per cent of the total frequency of symptoms of sickness.

Preventive Measures by Entrepreneurs

Out of the 19 entrepreneurs, 17 entrepreneurs had taken initiatives for the prevention of the sickness of their units. As for the other two entrepreneurs, one of them was unable to decide about the initiative he ought to have taken for preventing the sickness of his unit. The other entrepreneur was so much involved in the social works that he did not find time to initiate any preventive measure.

The remaining 17 entrepreneurs reported a variety of initiatives taken by them for preventing the sickness of their units. Two entrepreneurs had approached the KSFC to reschedule the repayment of term loans and six entrepreneurs had approached their financing bank branches for additional working capital facility. None of these entrepreneurs succeeded in their efforts because of the unhelpful attitude of officials. One person had deployed his own funds to overcome the financial problems but he could succeed only partly because of the paucity of funds with him. Five entrepreneurs had borrowed loans from the private parties to overcome their financial problems. While four of these entrepreneurs could succeed partly in overcoming their financial problems, one could not succeed at all because of the high rate of interest and poor borrowing capacity.

One entrepreneur had approached the Department of Industries and Commerce for the allotment of raw materials and the same entrepreneur had approached the Chief Minister also for getting sales-tax waived on his product. Though he could succeed in both of his endeavours, he could not succeed eve 1 then in preventing the sickness of his unit.

Three entrepreneurs had resorted to job-works but because of inadequate orders while two could succeed only partly, one could not succeed at all. Other three entrepreneurs had diversified their product-range but because of inadequate working capital while one could succeed only partly, two did not succeed at all. Another entrepreneurs could succeed partly in overcoming his problem by reducing his work-force.

In order to overcome marketing problem, one entrepreneur had appointed sales representatives and also a person for the recovery of dues. However, he could not succeed at all because of the poor purchasing power of farmer-customers and lack of funds with other customers. Another entrepreneur had made repeated representations to his parent unit for larger orders and better rates but he could not succeed at all. One entrepreneur had sought technical collaboration with a foreign firm and he could succeed only partly because of the shortage of working capital. Another entrepreneur had tried to lease out his unit for overcoming his financial problems but even that could not succeed.

Thus, out of 28 efforts made, only two had been fully successful, 10 partly successful, and 16 not successful at all. Though these entrepreneurs had succeeded to a varying extent in their endeavours to prevent the sickness of their units, none of them had been able to prevent the sickness of his unit.

Declaration of Sickness and Viability Studies

Out of the 19 sample sick SSI units, 14 units had been declared sick and 5 units were yet to be declared sick. Out of the 5 units, one unit, set up in 1963, remained closed during 1985-86 and 1986-87. The turnover of this unit was Rs. 92,000 in the year 1987-88 against the turnover of Rs. 600,000 in the initial year. The entrepreneur was no longer interested in retaining the unit.

Another unit that had not been declared sick was set up in 1980 but commercial production had commenced only in 1985-86. The working capital provided by its financing bank had been wasted on trial production and the bank had withdrawn working capital facility since

1982. The outstanding term loan in the year 1987-88 was Rs. 10,00,000 against the borrowed term loan of Rs. 600,000 from the KSFC in 1980. The unit was surviving on the basis of job-works and its annual turnover had been about Rs. 100,000 since 1985-86. Despite repeated requests by the entrepreneur to his bank and also repeated assurances by the concerned officials of his bank since 1985, the unit was yet to be declared sick.

The third unit, that was not declared sick, had been set up in the year 1975. This unit had become sick at the inception stage itself. In the initial year, turnover of this unit was Rs. 30,000 against a fixed investment of Rs. 182,000 and working capital limit of Rs. 95,000. Annual turnover of the unit was Rs. 18,000 in 1985-86, Rs. 34,000 in 1986-87, and Rs. 100,000 in 1987-88. The entrepreneur had borrowed a term loan of Rs. 141,000 in 1973 but had not been able to make any repayment against the borrowed term loan till 1988. The overdue working capital amount in 1988 was Rs. 287,000 against the sanctioned limit of Rs. 95,000. Despite repeated requests of the entrepreneur, his unit had not been declared sick. The entrepreneur informed that his bank had declared his unit unviable without having conducted any viability study.

The fourth unit that had not been declared sick by the financing bank was set up in 1980. This unit became sick in 1982 itself as it had runout of working capital fund. The unit had lost Rs. 120,000 in the course of its operation. Due to lack of repayment, the overdue working capital against the unit was Rs. 124,000 in the year 1987-88 against the sanctioned limit Rs. 60,000 by the bank in 1982. Since 1982, the unit had been surviving on the basis of job-work. The entrepreneur informed that his bank was not interested in declaring his unit sick as it was contemplating to file a legal suit for recovery.

The fifth unit that had not been declared sick was doing well till 1985-86. In 1986-87, its turnover came down to Rs. 14,75,000 from Rs. 27,00,000 in 1985-86, recording a decrease of about 45.4 per cent within a year. Further, its turnover had gone down to Rs. 445,000 in the year in 1987-88, recording a decrease of about 84.5 per cent over that in the year 1985-86. The ratio of turnover to total operational expenses had decreased from 1.4 in the year 1985-86 to 1.1 in the year 1987-88. While the share of manufacturing to total turnover was 96.3 per cent and that of job-work only 3.7 per cent in 1985-86, the respective shares were 51.7 per cent and 48.7 per cent in the year 1987-88. However, the financing bank had refused to declare his unit as sick. Thus, though the five units had not been declared sick by their banks, they deserved to be declared so.

Out of the remaining 14 sick units, 13 units had been declared sick by the concerned financing banks and/or institution. One unit, that had not been declared sick by the financing bank, had been declared sick by the Department of Industries and Commerce, Government of Karnataka in November 1987. This unit had been closed by the KSFC in 1985 and could be reopened in February 1986. However, it was closed again by the KSSIDC in November 1986 and it could be reopened in March 1987. According to the entrepreneur, while the KSFC had rescheduled the repayment of term loan, the financing bank had filed a legal suit for the recovery of due loan.

Out of the remaining 13 declared sick units, no initiative either for conducting viability study or for rehabilitation measures had been taken in the case of 3 units till 1988 though one of the three units had been declared sick in 1982, another in 1983, and the third one in 1986. In the case of remaining 10 units, the viability study of units had been completed. Out of these 10 units, the KSFC had conducted viability study of one unit, the SBI of four units, the SBM of one unit, the SISI of two units, the Technical and Consultancy Service Organisation of Karnataka (TECSOK) of one unit, and the SBI and the SISI together of one unit.

An analysis of the reported findings of the viability studies of 10 units revealed a number of causes of sickness. Among the different causes, marketing problems accounted for 31.8 per cent, inadequacy of working capital for 18.2 per cent, lack of raw materials for 13.6 per cent, and improper projections made by entrepreneurs for 9.1 per cent. Other causes were dependence of one buyer for marketing bulk of products, rejection of goods supplied, higher level of liabilities, accumulation of interests on borrowed term loan and working capital loan, diversion of working capital, high overheads, and high costs of production. Nine out of ten entrepreneurs were fully satisfied with the findings of viability studies and one entrepreneur was not satisfied at all with the findings. However, all the 10 units had been found to be viable.

The recommendations of viability studies for rehabilitation were reported by 8 out of 10 entrepreneurs. Two entrepreneurs informed that they were not aware of the recommendations regarding their units. Out of 18 frequency of recommendations the provision of additional working capital loan accounted for 6, and that of additional term loan for one. Other recommendations were conversion of overdue working capital loans into term loans, rescheduling of the repayment of term loans, funding of unpaid interests, realisation of interests incurred during the last three years in the next three years without any further interest, and the realisation of outstanding loans in the next seven years with an interest rate of 10 per cent, enhancing the duration of discounting bill facility from the existing 45 days to 75 days, and enhancement of the existing bill discounting limit of Rs. 300,000 to Rs. 500,000. Some other recommendations were that there should be a provision of margin money from the State Governmment, the Directorate of Supply and Disposal should provide marketing supports, the entrepreneur should get a partner capable of marketing the products, and the financing bank and KSFC should jointly undertake the responsibility of rehabilitation.

The lists of findings and recommendations may appear to be quite comprehensive but in reality they were no so with regard to individual units. On the basis of discussions with the individual entrepreneurs, it was found that the findings of viability studies were not based on any comprehensive analysis. The study teams generally based their findings on the verbal discussions they had with the concerned entrepreneurs. In fact, the entrepreneurs reported that whatever problems they told the study teams were generally accepted by them. By and large, the same was true with regard to the recommendations. Out of eight SSI units, a comprehensive package of rehabilitation measures seemed to have been recommended in the case of only one unit. In the case of other seven units, only half-backed adhoc-measures had been recommended.

Rehabilitation Programme

Out of 10 units for which viability studies had been completed, only 4 units had been covered under the rehabilitation programme till the time of survey in 1988. Out of the remaining six units, one unit had been declared sick in 1980, one in 1982, one in 1986, two in 1987, and one in 1988. The rehabilitation programmes were yet to be initiated for these units though viability studies were reported to have been completed for them. As for the four units which were under the rehabilitation programmes, the rehabilitation programmes had been started in the case of two units in 1986 and were expected to be completed by 1989 in the case of one unit and by 1990 in the case of the other unit. No time limit had been fixed for the completion of rehabilitation programme in the case of one unit for which rehabilitation programme had been started in the year 1987. In the case of fourth unit for which rehabilitation programme had been started in 1988, it was expected to be completed in 1991.

The details of the rehabilitation programmes, as furnished by the four entrepreneurs, revealed that the rehabilitation programmes were a bit comprehensive only in the case of two of the four units. In the case of remaining two units, the rehabilitation programmes appeared to be only some adhoc measures for giving some relief to the entrepreneurs. For example, the rehabilitation package in the case of one unit consisted of the sanction of additional working capital limit and a moratorium of one year for the repayment of loan. The concerned entrepreneur was only partly satisfied with both the measures because he found both of them inadequate. In the case of another unit, the rehabilitation package consisted of additional working capital limit and induction of a partner capable of marketing the products. The concerned entrepreneur was while fully satisfied with the provision of additional working capital limit, he was not at all happy with his bank's insistence on the induction of a new partner. Though the entrepreneur had to find a partner as it was a condition for the sanction of additional working capital limit, that partner could not come up to the expectation. The unit, after some improvement in the initial stage of rehabilitation, again slided back to the earlier position. The inducted partner had left the unit towards the end of 1987. In the case of third unit, the rehabilitation package consisted of (1) additional term loan from the KSFC, fresh working capital loan from the financing bank, and the conversion of overdue working capital loan into term loan. Though the entrepreneur was fully satisfied with all the three components of rehabilitation package, he informed that the concerned bank agreed for the rehabilitation of his unit not because of its concern for the unit but because he had been assured of adequate demand for his products by a large scale industrial firm for the next five years. In the case of fourth unit, the rehabilitation package consisted of conversion of all clean borrowings from bank into term loan, conversion of interest debited over the last two years into the interest free term loan, and additional working capital limit. The entrepreneur was fully satisfied with all the three measures.

As a whole, the rehabilitation process of sick units did not seem to be a systematic. Not much systematic efforts had been made to diagnose the causes of sickness of units, nor the rehabilitation packages seemed to be comprehensive. Out of 19 sick units, only two units appeared to have been under some sort of rehabilitation programme.

CASES OF SICKNESS SINCE INCEPTION

A variety of external factors as well as internal factors may cause and contribute to the sickness of a SSI unit at different stages of its life. However, in some cases a unit may become prone to sickness at the inception stage itself. Such a sickness can be attributed, generally to the faulty planning for the promotion and management of a unit. The promotion and management of a SSI unit requires a balanced integration of a variety of entrepreneurial and managerial functions. Any lop-sided emphasis or neglect may be because of the overconfidence of an entrepreneur in his own capability to manage his unit or taking for guaranted his financing bank, suppliers, customers and workers without understanding the commercial applications of borrowed capital, market dynamism and labour situation, etc. With the help of following cases, an attempt is being made to illustrate as to how a lop-sided emphasis on or neglect of one or more aspects of planning and management leads to the sickness of a SSI unit at its inception stage itself.

Overconfidence in Technical Competence without knowing Commercial Implications

Case-I

An entrepreneur, with a diploma in mechanical engineering and having work experience of four and a half-year in a large pencil (HB) manufacturing firm, set up his own pencil (HB) manufacturing unit in 1976. He borrowed term loan from the KSFC in 1974 for setting up of his unit. He was so confident of his technical competence that instead of buying plant and machinery he started making plant and machinery for his unit on his own. It took two years for him to develop his plant and machinery and production commenced only in 1976. By then, he had spent the borrowed working capital from bank on buying tools and accessories. While there was no commercial production for the first two years, his working capital had already got depleted and his liabilities had increased considerably. Thus, his indulgence in proving his technical competence without taking into account the commercial implications of borrowed capital had considerably weakened the financial strength of his unit in the beginning itself.

After production commenced, he had to face unfair competition in the marketing of his products by similar units in the neighbouring states of Maharashtra, Andhra Pradesh and Tamil Nadu on account of sales tax. While sales tax on pencil was exempted in these neighbouring states, it was not so in Karnataka. Also, he had problem in getting raw material (wood) because of the policy for protection of forests. Besides, he had to compete with the large pencil manufacturers who were supplying pencils on credit-basis. Further, with the popularity of ball pens, there had been a general decline in the demand for pencil. All these contributed to the sickness of his unit. His unit was declared sick in 1987.

Case-II

A mechanical engineer, who had worked for 17 years in a large scale public sector unit and rose from the position of an Engineer-Trainee to that of Manager (Product Design), set up his own machine tool accessories unit in 1975. His ambition was to introduce something new in the market, but he was not aware of its financial implications. After setting up of his unit, he had to spent considerable time on developing proto-type of his products and establishing their commercial viability. This led to financial crisis and his unit became sick the very next year after its establishment. The financial crisis created a vicious circle and neither the market potentiality could be tapped nor additional products could be introduced in the market. His unit was declared sick in 1980. Ultimately, his unit was closed in 1986 because of labour problems. However, a large public sector unit was interested in his product. Earlier, this product was being imported but subsequently the import of this item had been stopped. The public sector unit wanted the entrepreneur, therefore, to rectify the old imported items. The entrepreneur succeeded in rectifying them at one of his firends' unit. With this success, the public sector unit came forward to support the entrepreneur which led to the reopening of his unit in 1987. His unit was still sick at the time of survey.

Case-III

A physics professor had the ambition of producing NI-CD Battery in

India which was being imported. He was assured of proven technology for producing this item by a well known research and development corporation in the country. With this assurance, he set up his unit in 1980 by borrowing a term loan of Rs. 600,000 from the KSFC. However, the technology supplied did not succeed and borrowed working capital of Rs. 120,000 was wasted on trial production. This led to financial crisis and the financing bank stopped working capital facility in 1982. Till 1984-85, there was hardly any commercial production and the liabilities of the unit had increased considerably. In 1985-86, the unit started making plated-wire and since then it had been surviving, till the time of survey, on the basis of job-works. The financing bank had assured the entrepreneur in 1985 that his unit would be declared sick and rehabilitation assistance would be provided. However, the unit had neither been declared sick nor provided additional working capital by the financing bank till September, 1988. The entrepreneur informed that he had already got technical collaboration with a foreign firm and if working capital was provided, his unit could start the production of NI-CD Battery.

Inadequate Financial Support

Case-I

An electrical engineer, who had worked for 3 years as a maintenance-engineer in a paper factory and was electrical contractor for 5 years, set up his own GLS Lamp unit in 1977. According to the entrepreneur, price of machineries had got doubled between the time when order was placed and the time when machineries were delivered. To compensate the difference in price, the financing bank converted a part of sanctioned working capital limit into term loan without enhancing the limit. This led to the shortage of working capital in the beginning itself. Also, there was shortage of lead glass because of which the commencement of production was delayed considerably. At the same time, interest on bank loan was mounting. These initial financial problems affected future operation of the unit. After repeated requests to the financing bank for declaring the unit sick and providing rehabilitation facilities, the bank just clubbed all the outstanding loans, converted them into term loan, and opened a new account for the unit in 1982. The entrepreneur felt that the whole process was just an account adjustment excercise without giving any benefit to the unit.

The entrepreneur revealed that once he had received an order for supplying 100,000 bulbs to one organisation but could not execute the order because of the lack of working capital. He felt that had his bank given working capital, he would have made a profit of about Rs. 100,000 which might have proved to be a turning point for improving the health of his unit.

Case-II

An entrepreneur, educated only up to 7th standard and having 35 years of experience in High Frequency Plastic Welding Machinery, set up his own electrical engineering work unit in 1986 with the fixed investment of Rs. 280,000. He had borrowed a term loan of Rs. 200,000 from the KSFC. The main customer of the unit was to be a State Electricity Board (SEB). After he set up his unit, there was difference with the SEB about the rate for servicing transformers. A reasonable rate was approved by the SEB after a lot of discussion. The entrepreneur applied for working capital limit of Rs. 180,000 to a public sector bank after the rate was approved by the SEB. But the bank sanctioned a limit of only Rs. 30,000. With a very low working capital, operation of the unit was at a very low level. Also, there was a considerable delay in the payment by the SEB. Thus, the financial crisis became serious in the very beginning. This led to default in the payment of instalments to the KSFC and the KSFC, therefore, refused to recommend the case of unit for the sanction of a higher level of working capital limit to the bank. The unit became sick in the same year. However, it was only in May 1988 that the unit was declared sick by the KSFC and rehabilitation measures were proposed. But this was opposed by the bank as it had already filed a suit for recovery. The entrepreneur was no longer interested in reviving his unit and was planning to sell his plot and unit for the repayment of loan once court gave its verdict.

Wrong Product Selection

Case-I

A graduate in food technology set up his food processing unit in 1976. His unit was processing mushroom for the export purpose. However, he had difficulty in getting adequate raw mushrooms as the cost of mushroom was very high. Therefore, his turnover was low. In order to overcome this problem, he switched over to making instant food item, like *Sambhar* Powder. But after one and-a-half year, he realised that he had committed a mistake by switching over to the instant food items. To achieve the same turnover (value) level of mushroom processing, a very large quantity of instant food production was required. To achieve that level of production, an expansion of his unit was necessary and that required additional working space. Since his unit was located in a residential area, there was no space available for expansion. The operation level of his unit, therefore, remained very low and the unit was ultimately declared sick in 1980. In 1982, a shed in an industrial estate was allotted to him but it took three years for him to get power connection. As soon as that shed was allotted to him, his bank came forward to revive his unit. However, the bank took 3 years to consider his proposal and he could get additional loan only in October 1986. The bank was insisting that he should get a partner who would stand guarantee for him and help him in marketing. The entrepreneur could manage to get such a partner in March 1987. But, his partner could not be of much help in marketing of his products. His unit became sick once again. Later on in the same year, he got an order of Rs. 12,50,000 from the defence department but he could not execute the complete order because his bank delayed the disbursement of working capital loan for 15 days. At the time of survey, the current liabilities of his unit were about Rs. 550,000 and assets were worth Rs. 150,000.

Case-II

An engineering graduate, having 8 years of experience in management and sales in the private companies, set up an ancillary unit for manufacturing coils and transformers, and electronic assembly in 1975. After setting up his unit, he was in a fix as the parent unit did not allot a *dedicated item* for manufacturing to his unit. In the first year, the parent unit assured that his unit would be given order for supplying 100, 000 coils but ultimately it placed order for only 38,000 coils — which was not sufficient for a viable operation of his unit throughout the year. Even in the subsequent years, no *dedicated item* was allotted to the unit and parent unit kept placing order on an adhoc basis. Because of this, no planned development of unit could take place. Also, his unit was closed frequently because of the non-supply of basic and critical raw materials by the parent unit on a regular basis. Thus, the unit was in problem from the very beginning because of the non-allotment of a dedicated item, adhoc and inadequate order from the parent unit and irregular supply of raw materials. In the very second year, the entrepreneur found that his unit had acquired the symptoms of sickness. However, he could manage somehow till 1986-87, by reducing his work force and resorting to job-works. But in 1987-88 his unit was in acute problem and annual turnover came down from Rs. 800,000 in 1986-87 to Rs. 450,000. His unit was declared sick by his bank in January 1988, and rehabilitation measures were started in February 1988.

Entrepreneurial Incompetence

Case-I

An engineer set up a unit for manufacturing electrical transformers in 1980. His unit was a partnership concern and he was dependent on his working-partner for technical and marketing support. However, his partner left the unit in 1981. The entrepreneur was not able to get a suitable replacement and he was not confident of his own competence. He, therefore, resorted to job-works. Even then his bank had enhanced his working capital limit from Rs. 40,000 in 1980 to Rs. 60,000 in 1982. However, the entrepreneur lost the working capital of Rs. 60,000 borrowed from his bank in running the unit. At the time of survey, the outstanding working capital loan against the unit was Rs. 124,000 as he had not repayed the withdrawn amount. In 1984, one of his customers introduced him to a private large scale unit and an agreement for doing job-works was finalised. Since then, that large scale unit had been his sole customer till the time of survey. The unit had been just surviving on the orders received from this sole customer. The annual turnover of unit was Rs. 25,000 in 1980 and it had gone up to only Rs. 85,000 in 1987-88. The entrepreneur revealed that his bank was not willing to declare his unit sick as it was interested in filing recovery suit in the court. The entrepreneur too was not very enthusiastic about reviving his unit. He observed that if situation got further deteriorated, he would dispose of the unit and look for a job. However, he was toying with the idea of setting up a new unit for which he had already got a project report. But the big question mark was the availability of finance for setting up a new unit.

Summary

The analysis of information furnished by 19 out of 22 sick SSI units revealed that a unit may become sick at any stage of its life. Most of the entrepreneurs had noticed the symptoms of sickness of their units on their own. Mounting liabilities and shrinking working capital were the major symptoms of sickness. Most of the entrepreneurs had taken some or other initiatives in order to prevent the sickness of their units but none of them could, ultimately, succeed. No systematic approach seemed to have been followed for declaring a unit sick. In the case of some of the units that had been declared sick a few years back, no initiative had been taken either for conducting viability study or for extending rehabilitation facilities. An analysis of the findings of viability studies and the recommended rehabilitation measures revealed that neither the viability studies had been conducted in a systematic manner, nor the rehabilitation packages were comprehensive.

A few select case of the sick units that had acquired the symptoms of sickness at the inception stage itself revealed that these units had become sick mainly because of (i) lop-sided emphasis in the planning and management, (ii) inadequate financial support, (iii) wrong product selection, and (iv) entrepreneurial incompetence.

9

TURNING POINTS
Cases of Select Sample Units

A small entrepreneur operates in a business environment which is quite dynamic. Also, he has to depend on a number of government agencies, financial agencies, and private suppliers and customers for the performance of his enterprise. Besides, he has to operate within limited resources at his command. He, therefore, has to be extra-vigilant. He has to keep himself not only alert enough to be able to notice the signals sent by his business environment but also prepared to take the advantages of favourable conditions and to resist and minimise the impact of unfavourable conditions on his enterprise.

The performance of an enterprise depends on a variety of external factors as well as internal factors. The external factors such as change in government policy, economic growth, economic recession, price fluctuation, increase in demand on account of certain developments, shortage of some critical inputs, natural calamities and spread of disease, etc. are generally considered to be beyond the control of an entrepreneur. The internal factors, like plants and machinery, manpower, and finances, etc. of an enterprise are supposed to be within the control of an entrepreneur. The external factors may provide opportunites and favourable conditions for the growth of an enterprise during a certain period or at a particular point of time. The same factors may also create adverse conditions that may lead to stagnation or even demise of an enterprise.

A small entrepreneur, depending on his ability and managerial competence, can exercise full control over his internal factors so as to take full advantage of the opportunities and favourable conditions. In an adverse situation, an entrepreneur may, with his ability, managerial competence and control over his internal factors, resist and minimise the impact of unfavourable conditions on his enterprise. If going becomes too tough, he may adapt himself to the changed business environment and effect such changes in his business strategies as are essential for the survival and progress of his enterprise. In other words, a good entrepreneur may be down for some time but he cannot be out of his business. Only when an entrepreneur ignores or fails to recognise the signals sent by his business environment and is unable to exercise full control over his internal factors that his enterprise stagnates becomes sick or gets liquidated.

Whether an entrepreneur is able to harness the favourable conditions to the advantage of his enterprise or succumbs to the unfavourable conditions, there is bound to be, in either case, a sharp change in the course of the performance of his enterprise. These changes may be for better or for worse as per the case. Such changes can be termed as 'turning points' in the life of an enterprise. However, it is not necessary that if an enterprise has experienced a turning-point for better or worse, at a particular point of time, it would never get reversed in future. It would depend on the ability, competence and experience of entrepreneur that would determine whether he succeeds or succumbs to in future. In some cases, the very failure for the first time may prove to be a pillar of success in future, provided the entrepreneur has learnt the necessary lessons from his previous failure and has equipped himself for the tasks to be performed in future. Only when an entrepreneur fails to learn lessons from his past mistakes and is unable to take the remedial measures that the failure at one point of time goes on perpetuating itself with growing intensification in future, leading to the sickness and death of his enterprise.

It is quite evident from the cases of turning points experienced by some of the sample SSI units presented in this chapter, that the performance of an enterprise neither follows the same direction nor moves at the same pace for ever. The failure of an entrepreneur at one point of time does not mean that he is doomed for ever. There is always a possibility that he may once again rise and march ahead provided he is able to overcome his earlier shortcomings. Similarly, an entrepreneur successful at a particular point of time need not remain successful for ever if he does not keep himself abreast with his changing business environment and prepared for the inevitable in future. Some of the sample units that could be classified as very successful and successful had faced teething problems and were at the verge of demise once upon a time. Similarly, some of the units that were sick or whose performance was not upto expectation were flourishing once upon a time. The following cases of turning points are presented with a view to illustrate these situations. Such illustrations could be useful for the entrepreneurs as well as others, like, financing agencies, promotional agencies, concerned government departments, policy makers and academicians.

CASES: VERY SUCCESSFUL GROUP

Product change and Diversification

Case-I

An entrepreneur, with a Diploma in Tool and Die-making and having an experience of 9 years as a foreman in the same line, set-up a tool manufacturing unit in 1971. The initial investment on plant and machinery was only Rs. 16,000. In the first year, only 3 workers were employed in the unit and annual turnover was only Rs. 18,000. The unit was facing teething problems in the initial stage and therefore, the entrepreneur switched over from tool making to job-works. However, even resorting to job-works was not of much help. In 1974, the entrepreneur took a decision to change his product line from tool making to manufacturing industrial valves, for which there was a good demand. This proved to be a turning point for the progress of his unit. In the very first year of this shift, his unit made 100 per cent profit. This gave a lot of encouragement to the entrepreneur and he started diversifying his product-range by developing a variety of industrial valves of different dimensions. By 1987-88, his unit had become a leading industrial valve manufacturing unit in the country. The fixed investment had gone up to Rs. 21,25,000 and annual turnover to Rs. 22.5 million. The number of persons employed had gone up to 48. Also, the entrepreneur had set-up another unit ancillary to the main unit. Further, he was negotiating for technical collaboration with a company from the United States of America for setting up a third unit.

Case-II

A post-graduate woman entrepreneur, trained in food technology and having an experience of 3 years as a consultant for product development, set-up her own food processing unit in 1981. The initial fixed investment in the unit was Rs. 450,000 and 10 persons were employed. The annual turnover was only Rs. 25,000 in the first year. Her unit was processing only one item-tamarind powder which was not adequate for full utilisation of the installed capacity. In 1982-83, the entrepreneur made efforts to get technical know-how for processing food ingredients for the requirements of defence department. She succeeded in her efforts and that proved to be the turning point for the progress of her unit. She diversified the product-range, and in 1985, she became a major supplier to the defence department. Her unit had a record growth of 100 per cent in that year. By 1987-88, the fixed investment on plant and machinery in her unit had gone up to Rs. 850,000, annual turnover to Rs. 1700,000 and the number of persons employed to 25.

Intervention by Competent Official

Case-I

An entrepreneur, with a diploma in engineering and having experience of 25 years of which 22 years in a public sector telephone manufacturing unit, set-up a unit ancillary to the same telephone manufacturing unit in 1974. His unit was manufacturing and assembling receiver capsule for the parent unit. The initial fixed investment on plant and machinery was Rs. 230,000 and annual turnover was Rs. 100,000. His unit was doing well till 1983 but went under stagnation in 1984. Because of the change in quality requirement of the parent unit, the receiver capsules supplied by his unit were rejected. Subsequently, his bank stopped giving financial support to his unit due to the rejection and his unit ultimately became sick. However, the entrepreneur did not give up. He invested his own resources for creating additional facility at his unit for improving quality of his product to the level of requirement of his parent unit. After that, he rectified the shortcomings of the rejected goods and invited the concerned official of his parent unit for inspection of the additional facility created and the goods rectified. The concerned official found the facility and goods upto their satisfaction and his parent unit was ready to accept goods on sample basis. But, the entrepreneur was not ready to supply his goods on a sample basis. In the meanwhile, the Telecommunication Department of Government of India had been asking persistently to supply telephone receivers. Also, a higher level official from the corporate office of the parent unit was posted as the Executive Director at the production unit. This official used to visit the industrial estate earlier quite frequently and was well familiar with the problems of ancillary units. The entrepreneur presented the case of his unit to this official and his intervention led to the solution of the entrepreneur's problem. The parent unit not only placed substantial order but also enhanced the rate. Following this, his financing bank too agreed to resume financial support to the unit. Thus, the intervention of a competent official proved to be the turning point for the unit. Since then, this ancillary unit had been doing very well. The annual turnover of the unit, which was only Rs. 500,000 in the year 1985-86, increased to Rs. 2, 200,000 in the year 1987-88.

Case-II

An engineering unit was established by two engineer brothers (partners) in the year 1968 soon after they had completed their education. Both the brothers had done their graduation in mechanical engineering and set-up this unit without having any work experience. Their unit was not doing well in the initial period and a few instalments of the repayment of loans to the NSIC had been defaulted. The NSIC was about to seize the unit in 1974. The financial position of entrepreneurs was so bad that they had almost lost the hope of retaining their unit. However, a Regional Manager of the State Bank of India who was convinced came forward to take over all the liabilities of the unit without demanding any margin from the entrepreneur. Thus, with the intervention of a competent bank official, the entrepreneurs could retain their unit which became a great source of encouragement for them. It was indeed a turning-point for the unit. The entrepreneurs were determined to succeed in future. Since then the unit had been doing well. Within a few years, the entrepreneurs were able to repay all the liabilities. By 1987-88, the fixed investment in the unit had gone up from Rs. 100,000 in 1968 to Rs. 20,00,000; the annual turnover had gone up from Rs. 60,000 in 1968 to Rs. 40,00,000; and the number of persons employed from 8 to 35.

Management

Case-I

A graduate, having a diploma in Marketing Management, set-up his unit for manufacturing control cubicles and fabrication items in 1974. Before setting up his unit, he had worked for 11 years as Marketing Manager, Senior Accounts Executive and Manager — Public Relations in certain private companies. When he went to set-up his unit, two large scale units had assured him of buying most of his products. However, the marketing arrangement did not materialise to the full extent and his unit became a losing concern. By 1978, his unit had become sick.

The entrepreneur sought help of a consultant for improving the health of his unit but the consultant did not find the job remunerative enough and backed out. However, the entrepreneur started creating data base of his unit on his own. For the first time in 1978, he got the balance sheet of his unit prepared and tried to understand the same. He could realise as to how serious was the problem of his unit. Accordingly, he worked out strategies for improving the health of his unit. He began doing product audit of his unit. Through this, he could know the product-items that did not give sufficient profit margins. He abandoned the production of such items though it meant idling or scrapping of a considerable portion of investment. At the same time, he gave priority to the production of such items for which tooling requirement was not much and customers themselves supplied materials. In other words, he adopted the strategy of being loyal to his business rather than being loyal to a particular product item. These strategies helped him in reducing the losses of his unit for the first time in 1979.

Next, he diversified his product-range into major multi-component assemblies (driver's cabin and seat) and off loaded small product-items to some other SSI units. Further, he shifted the focus of monitoring the performance of his unit from on the size of turnover to on the proportion of value added. This self-learning of managing his business proved to be a turning point for the progress of his unit. By 1987-88, the fixed investment in his unit had gone up from Rs. 328,000 in the initial year to Rs. 16,49,139, the annual turnover from Rs. 280,000 to Rs. 53,51,000 and the number of persons employed had gone up from 18 to 58.

Growing Industrialisation: Increasing Demand

Case-I

An electronic engineer, without any previous work experience, set-up an electroplating unit in 1974. In the early 1970s, a major industrial estate was established in Bangalore. Because of this facility, a large number of small scale electroplating units were set-up within a short period. Most of these units were dependent on orders received from the public sector units in and around Bangalore. Therefore, there was a stiff competition among the small scale electroplating units till 1980 and this entrepreneur's unit was no exception. However, a major industrial centre at Hosur, near Bangalore, had come up by 1980. The emergence of this centre created a lot of demand for electroplating which proved to be a turning point for the progress of this unit. The fixed investment in the unit, in 1980, was only Rs. 234,000 which had gone up to Rs. 12,29,000 by June 1982. During the same period, the annual turnover of the unit increased from Rs. 9,59,000 to Rs. 21,89,000 and the profit earned increased from Rs. 59,000 to Rs. 2,53,000. Since then, the unit had been making very good progress. By March 1988, the fixed investment in the unit had increased from Rs. 89,000 in 1975 to Rs. 35, 52,000, the annual turnover from Rs. 54,000 to Rs. 117,74,000 and the number of persons employed from 6 to 140. During the same period, the profit earned by the unit had gone up from Rs. 12,000 to Rs. 11,95,000.

CASES: SUCCESSFUL GROUP

Certain Developments Causing Increase in Demand

Case-I

A matriculate who had worked as a mechanic in an institute for 26 years, set-up his own unit for servicing electrical equipments in 1978 at Mysore. To begin with, his unit was quite modest. The fixed investment in his unit was Rs. 10,000 and annual turnover in the first year was Rs. 25,000. Only 3 persons were employed in the unit and those too were his own family members. There was not much progress till 1983. *In 1984-85, a TV Relay centre was established at Mysore. The introduction of TV relay caused demand for control equipments and DC power supply units. The entrepreneur took advantage of this opportunity. Though he was not able to get working capital support from any bank, he could mobilise his own funds for making additional products to meet the new demands. This proved to be the turning point for the progress of his unit. Since then his unit had been doing well.

Once the performance of his unit improved, a bank agreed to provide working capital support. The entrepreneur, therefore, changed his earlier bank and that helped him overcoming his working capital problem. By 1987-88, the fixed investment in his unit had gone up to Rs. 1,25,000, annual turnover had gone up to Rs. 750,000, and the number of persons employed had gone up to 10. The entrepreneur was quite optimistic about the future and as trying to get a Japanese collaboration for assembling video cassette recorders and video cassette players.

Case-II

An entrepreneur, who had post-graduate degree in food technology and had worked as food analyst in Kuwait for 9 years, set-up his own unit for manufacturing rubber latex and allied products in 1980. In the initial year, the turnover of his unit was Rs. 344,000. The Government of India had organised ASIAD in New Delhi in 1982. According to the entrepreneur, sports activities in India became quite popular following the ASIAD and that led to many fold increase in the demand of his products. Thus, the holding of ASIAD in 1982 proved to be turning point for the progress of his unit. Later on, with the spread of AIDS (disease) and its knowledge, the demand for his product (rubber latex) further increased. By 1987-88, the annual turnover of his unit had gone up to about Rs. 53,00,000 without any appreciable rise in the fixed investment.

Technological Change and Innovation

Case-I

A post-graduate entrepreneur, who had received intensive training in financial management and had an experience of 16 years as accountant executive, set-up a fasteners and allied products manufacturing unit in 1975. The initial fixed investment was Rs. 675,000, the initial annual turnover was only Rs. 80,000 and only 6 persons were employed in the unit. In 1977, the entrepreneur changed his technology from cold forging to hot forging and replaced crude machinery by precision machinery. This proved to be a turning point for the progress of his unit. By 1987-88, the fixed investment in his unit had gone up to Rs. 10,25,000, annual turnover to Rs. 22,00,000 and the number of persons employed to 50.

Case-II

A unit for manufacturing special purpose machines and precision tools was set-up as a partnership concern by three entrepreneurs in 1976. All the three entrepreneurs were mechanical engineers and had 11-12 years of experience in large scale public sector units. In 1978, a public sector unit, the Hindustan Machine Tools, enquired from the entrepreneurs as to whether they would be able to make tungsten wire drawing machines for its lamp unit. The entrepreneurs accepted it as a challenge to their technical competence and succeeded in their endevours. This proved to be a turning point for the progress of their unit. The customers started coming from all over India. The annual turnover of the unit, which was only Rs. 127,000 in 1978, increased to Rs. 625,000 in 1979 and to Rs. 15,00,000 in 1985. The fixed investment which was Rs. 761,700 in the initial year had gone up to Rs. 13,71,700 in 1987-88. However, the entrepreneurs revealed that the size of business was not sufficient for them and, therefore, they were planning for expansion and modernisation of the unit to make it a medium scale unit.

Case-III

An entrepreneur, having education up to 12th standard, had worked as an operator in a public sector unit for 4 and a-half-years and as a tool room superintendent in a multi-national unit for 18 years. After having an experience of more than 22 years, the entrepreneur acquired a sick SSI unit (set-up for casting ferrous and non-ferrous items) in 1978. At the time of acquisition of the unit, fixed investment in the unit was Rs. 250,000. The annual turnover in the first year after acquisition was Rs. 300,000. The performance of unit was so-so till 1983. In 1984, a multi-national company asked the entrepreneur to develop two import substitution items–mechanical parts of high voltage switch gear. The entrepreneur took it as challenge and succeeded in developing the substitution items. This proved to be a turning point for the progress of his unit. By 1987-88, the fixed investment in his unit had gone up to Rs. 20,12,000 and the annual turnover to Rs. 20,00,000.

Product Change and Diversification

Case-I

An ancillary unit for manufacturing fabrication items was set-up as a partnership concern by two entrepreneurs in 1974. Both of them had diploma in mechanical engineering and they had received technical training, entrepreneurship training and management training. While one of the entrepreneurs did not have any experience, the other had an experience of 16 years. He had received technical training for two years in the Federal Republic of Germany and had worked as programme and planning engineer in the United Kingdom for 8 years.

Till 1984-85 the annual turnover of their unit used to be in the range of Rs. 300,000 to Rs. 400,000. In 1985, they diversified their product from mere fabrication to complete assembly. This proved to be a turning point for the progress of their unit. In the very next year, the annual turnover of the unit increased to Rs. 12,00,000 and it had gone up to Rs. 15,00,000 by 1987-88.

Case-II

An entrepreneur, having a degree in mechanical engineering, had received training for nine months abroad. He had graduated from the level of an apprentice to tool room manager during his work experience of 16 years in a public sector unit. He set-up his own unit for manufacturing cutting tools in 1973, with an initial fixed investment of Rs. 3,36,000. The annual turnover of the unit in the first year was only Rs. 64,000. He realised in 1976, that there was not much demand for tool room products and because of that the installed capacity of his unit remained under utilised. He, therefore, replaced some of the old machinery and switched over from manufacturing to doing job-works in 1978. This proved to be a turning-point for the progress of his unit. By 1987-88, the fixed investment in his unit had gone up to Rs. 10,81,000 and the annual turnover had gone up to Rs. 800,000.

Market Diversification

Case-I

An entrepreneur, with education up to 12th standard and having work experience of 2 and a-half years as security and maintenance officer in a private company, set-up an ancillary unit for manufacturing control equipments in 1965. Till 1980, his unit was not doing well because of inadequate demand from the parent unit. In 1981, the entrepreneur finalised and entered into a marketing arrangement with a large scale public sector unit. This proved to be a turning point for the progress of his unit. The unit achieved the highest turnover of Rs. 20,00,000 in 1983-84 against the annual turnover of Rs. 30,000 in the first year.

Case-II

An entrepreneur, with education up to 12th standard, had worked as a clerk for 9 years in a public sector bank. Before setting up his unit, he had received training for a brief period in the buyer unit. He set-up his own unit for manufacturing Valve Guides in 1979 with an initial fixed investment of Rs. 308,000. The annual turnover in the first year was Rs. 200,000. Till 1983, his unit was just surviving as it was dependent on a sole buyer. However, in 1984, there was a strike for six months in the sole buyer-unit which caused acute marketing problem for his unit. As a result, his unit incurred a loss of Rs. 360,000 in that year. Once the sole buyer-unit was re-opened, his unit started recovering but the entrepreneur had already started making efforts for the diversification of market for his products. His success in the diversification of market proved to be the turning point for the progress of his unit. At the time of survey, his unit had 9 major customers against the sole-buyer earlier. By 1987-88, the fixed investment in his unit had gone up to Rs. 863,000 and the annual turnover had gone up to Rs. 14,50,000 against Rs. 2,00,000 in the first year. After the diversification of market, the demand for his products had increased so much that the entrepreneur had to set-up two additional units in the same product-line, one in 1987 and the other in 1988. Even then, he was finding it difficult to meet the demand.

CASES: AVERAGE GROUP

Slump in Demand

Case-I

Two brothers, one having education up to matriculation and the other having education up to 12th standard, set-up a biscuit and confectionery unit in 1970. Both the brothers had received technical and entrepreneurship trainings. The initial fixed investment in the unit was Rs. 6,50,000. In the first year, the annual turnover of unit was Rs. 40,00,000 and 35 persons were employed in the unit. There used to be power-cut for such units in Karnataka till 1977 and it was lifted in

1978. As a result of adequate power availability since 1978, there was a substantial increase in the production and the entrepreneurs could expand market for their products. The demand was so high that they were unable to meet the same in 1980, 1981 and 1982 in spite of the fact that there was 100 per cent utilization of the installed capacity of their unit.

Anticipating that the demand for their products would continue to be high, they bought additional plants and machinery and substantially enhanced the installed capacity of their unit from 2640 tonnes to 5400 tonnes a year. However, the number of biscuit manufacturing units in Karnataka increased from 5 in 1983 to over 60 in 1985. This resulted in stiff competition leading to the under-utilization of installed capacity of their unit. The turnover was fluctuating from year to year. The annual turnover of their unit was Rs. 1,48,00,000 in 1985-86; it came down to Rs. 1,18,00,000 in 1986-87 and went up again to Rs. 1,59,00,000 in 1987-88.

Case-II

An entrepreneur, with a bachelor degree in mechanical engineering and having an experience of four and a-half-years set-up a food processing unit (Dehydrated Green Pepper) in 1976 as a partnership concern. The unit was set-up with an initial fixed investment of Rs. 8,45,000. In the first year, the annual turnover was Rs. 9,99,000 and 20 persons were employed in the unit. In the first three years, the performance of his unit was good because of good demand for his products in some foreign countries. Anticipating that there would be good demand for his products in the fourth year as well, the entrepreneur produced goods worth Rs. 35,00,000. However, there was a big slump in demand for his products in the fourth year and his unit could receive order worth only Rs. 2,00,000 in that year. This proved to be a turning point for his unit in 1978-79. It took another 3 years for him to sell the products of fourth year. In the meanwhile, his bank withdrew financial support and his unit was declared sick but no rehabilitation facilities were extended to his unit. His partners too deserted the unit and it became a proprietorship concern. Following this, the entrepreneur went for the development of a new product and could succeed in standardizing a perfumery extraction item in 1983. This proved to be another turning point for his unit and since then his unit had been doing well. Later in 1987, another new instant food product was introduced for which there had been good demand from the defence departments. Thus, the unit had almost recovered and the annual turnover, which was Rs. 7,00,000 in 1985, increased to Rs. 17,00,000 in 1986 and further to Rs. 24,00,000 in 1987.

Case-III

A matriculate, with diploma in mechanical engineering and having an experience of 8 years as a foreman and supervisor in a large scale public sector unit, set-up an ancillary unit for doing job-works in 1960. The initial fixed investment in his unit was Rs. 85,000 and annual turnover in the first year was Rs. 3,50,000. Later on, additional machinery were added for manufacturing machine. However, there was very limited demand from the parent unit in the first half of 1970s. The entrepreneur, therefore, started exploring outside market and could get good demand for his product in a private large scale unit. The demand in the beginning was so good that the entrepreneur was asked by the customer unit to have full facility at his unit. With assured demand, the entrepreneur went ahead for creating additional facilities at his unit by borrowing Rs. 2,80,000 from his bank. But soon after the expansion of his unit, his new customer stopped giving order to his unit. This proved to be a turning point for his unit. As the interest and instalment amount was mounting, the branch manager of his bank stopped the operation of his account. This led to a variety of problems and entrepreneur was so up set that he wanted to sell his unit to repay the bank loan. However, he was able to open a new account with another bank branch. Through this, he could get some help to keep his unit running. Incidentally, he received an order worth Rs. 4,00,000 from a sister concern of his parent unit in 1977. It was a sheer coincidence that a new manager had come to his earlier bank branch. The new manager called the entrepreneur and permitted him to operate his old account after some discussion. These two incidents proved to be a turning point for his unit. With execution of this order, his unit started recovering and he could clear all the bank loans within a period of two years.

Illness of Entrepreneur

Case-I

A matriculate, with diploma in mechanical engineering, set-up a foundry unit in 1967 with the initial fixed investment of Rs. 58,000. In the first year, the annual turnover was Rs. 25,000 and 15 persons were employed in his unit. The entrepreneur met with a serious accident in 1972 and he could not look after the functioning of his unit for long. As a result, while production at his unit was greatly affected, the overheads continued to be as usual for quite some time. It took along time for the unit to recover and the turnover remained low. The unit was surviving by doing job-works. The annual turnover had increased from 1,25,000 in 1985-86 to Rs. 1,45,000 in 1986-87 and it declined to Rs. 90,000 in 1987-88. Only 8 persons were employed in 1987-88 against 15 persons in the initial year.

CASES: SICK GROUP

Rejection

Case-I

Two brothers, one graduate and having an experience of four years as a sales assistant in a private company and the other having an experience of 10 years in his own business, set-up a unit for manufacturing corrugated sheet in 1981. The initial fixed investment in the unit was Rs. 2,76,000 and 10 persons were employed in the first year. The annual turnover in the very first year was Rs. 24,00,000. Their unit did very well till 1983-84. However, there was a lot of rejection of the goods supplied in 1984-85 because of the low quality of raw materials. This proved to be the turning point for the unit toward sickness. A substantial amount of loan instalments to the KSFC could not be paid by the unit. The KSFC, therefore, closed the unit in 1985. Later on, the entrepreneurs could pay Rs. 80,000 to the KSFC and their unit was re-opened in February 1986. But, they had not paid shed-rent to the KSSIDC amounting to Rs. 70,000. The KSSIDC, therefore, closed the unit in November 1986. Again, the entrepreneurs could pay Rs. 25,000 to the KSSIDC and got their unit re-opened in March 1987. The entrepreneur had a dispute with the KSSIDC as it had calculated the overdue rent on the basis of revised rate (Rs. 2900 a month) instead of the old rate (Rs. 900 a month). The entrepreneurs approached the KSFC and their bank branch for the rescheduling of outstanding loans. While the KSFC agreed and rescheduled the outstanding loan the concerned bank did not oblige the entrepreneurs and filed a legal suit against the unit. The unit had been declared sick by the Directorate of industries, Government of Karnataka in November 1987 and recommended for rehabilitation to the concerned bank branch. However, the concerned bank branch had not taken any action for the rehabilitation of unit till the time of survey. The annual turnover of the unit was only Rs. 3,00,000 in 1987-88 as against Rs. 24,00,000 in the very first year.

Case-II

An entrepreneur, with a bachelor degree in mechanical engineering and having six years of experience in a SSI unit, acquired the same SSI unit in 1976. At the time of acquisition, the unit had a fixed investment of Rs. 1,00,000 and it was manufacturing clamping elements. In the first year after acquisition, annual turnover of the unit was Rs. 1,75,000 and 12 persons were employed. In 1983-84, the entrepreneur went for a major expansion of his unit by investing Rs. 5,00,000 in plant and machinery for manufacturing bungs for LPG (cooking gas) cylinders. He used to take a bar stock roll, turn it and supply it to a LPG company. Later on, the ISI (Indian Standards Institute) made the forging of this component compulsory but the material suggested by the ISI was not of a forging quality. A thin hairline-crack used to be there causing rejection to the extent of 60 per cent of bungs supplied. This proved to be a turning point for the unit. The entrepreneur had to sell the rejected bungs as scrap. Ultimately, he had to stop the manufacture of bungs. The special purpose machine acquired for making bungs became idle as it could not be used for any other purpose. All these led to a shortage of working capital. Further, his bank made his account non-operational which caused non-production of other established items. All these led to the sickness of his unit in 1985 and his bank declared his unit sick in December 1986. After the declaration of his unit as sick, he sold the special-purpose-machine for making bungs and deposited the realised amount with the KSFC. By this time, his bank branch appreciated the problem of his unit. With the cooperation of bank and the KSFC, his unit was under rehabilitation.

Non-Realisation of Bills and Slump in Demand

Case-I

An engineer, with an experience of 3 years in a private large scale company, set-up a unit for manufacturing aluminium collapsible chips in 1973. The initial fixed investment in the unit was Rs. 3,00,000 and 15 persons were employed in the first year. His unit was doing well till 1982-83. By then, the fixed investment in his unit had gone up to Rs. 17,00,000 and the annual turnover had gone up to Rs. 32,00,000. His major customer was a tooth paste manufacturing company which was buying about 70 per cent of his products (tubes). In 1983, there was a bulk rejection of tooth paste exported by the buyer company which meant the rejection of tubes worth Rs. 10,00,000 supplied by the entrepreneur. This proved to be a turning point towards the sickness of his unit. He could not realise the bills of Rs. 10,00,000 for long from this company and his unit became sick due to the acute shortage of working capital. Though his bank agreed for the rehabilitation of his unit in 1987, the entrepreneur could not revive his unit as it had lost all its customers. His unit's liabilities had gone up to Rs. 29,00,000 while the assets were worth only Rs. 25,00,000. The entrepreneur too had lost interest in reviving his unit and it was taken over by a different management in 1988.

Case-II

A matriculate with diploma in mechanical engineering and having an experience of 5 years as production engineer in a firm, set-up his unit for doing job-work in 1971. The initial fixed investment in the unit was Rs. 1,90,000. The annual turnover in the first year was Rs. 50,000 and 13 persons were employed. His unit started manufacturing axles of trailer in 1977. There was a good demand for axles till 1982. In the same year, production was diversified to the manufacture of complete trailers. There was good demand for trailers as well till 1985. However, there was a sharp decline in the demand for trailers since 1986 because of drought conditions in Karnataka. In order to overcome the decline in demand for trailers, his unit started producing another item, *Gober*-gas plants against government orders. However, the State Government did not lift a large number of ordered *Gobar*-gas plants that had already been manufactured by the unit. The main reason for the non-lifting of ordered plant was that when the government withdrew the provision of subsidies, farmers were not interested in installing *Gobar*-gas plants. Because of this, substantial working capital fund remained blocked. Earlier, another customer had not paid Rs. 1,50,000 for trailer components supplied in 1985. All these led to an acute shortage of working capital and production was affected very much. His unit ultimately became sick but his bank branch refused to declare it sick. At the time of survey, his unit was surviving by taking recourse to job works.

Diversion of Funds and Neglect

Case-I

An entrepreneur, with education up to 7th standard and having an experience of 11 years as an electric motor winder in a private firm, set-up his own unit for welding transformers and rewinding of motors in 1962. Though the entrepreneur had only limited formal education, he appeared to be a well-read person. As such, the limited formal education was not a handicap for him. The initial fixed investment in the unit was Rs. 30,000. In the first year, annual turnover of his unit was Rs. 2, 50,000 and 30 persons were employed. His unit was doing very well till early 1970s. The entrepreneur revealed that there was a time when his living standard was pretty high and he used to maintain two cars. In 1972, he started making efforts for getting a foreign collaboration to manufacture switch gear. He was concentrating his efforts on securing that foreign collaboration and neglected the management of his unit. For getting collaboration, the entrepreneur had been to the USA once and to Europe thrice. He had spent about Rs. 1,50,000 of his working capital funds on these visits. In the meanwhile, his unit had lost a major customer in 1974. Also, he was very much involved in social work in the community and did not pay adequate attention to the management of his unit. All these affected the performance of his unit. Besides, he did not succeed in getting the foreign collaboration. With deteriorating performance of his unit after 1972, his unit's liabilities went on increasing and he was unable to repay the bank loans. As a result, his relationship with his bank branch was affected and the working capital facility was withdrawn. His unit was declared sick by the Directorate of Industries, Government of Karnataka in 1978 and by his bank in 1982. His unit was sick even at the time of this survey and it had been surviving only by doing job-works.

Summary

From the presentation of the cases of turning points of select sample units, it is obvious that the quality of entrepreneurship is the key-factor in determining the course of a small enterprise. In the very successful group, the select units had faced the problems of limited demand for products, rejection of goods, poor performance, financial constraints and stiff competition, etc. However, the entrepreneurs, belonging to this group, could change the course of their enterprises by changing and diversifying their product-renage, improving the quality of their products, deploying their own resources, changing their business strategies, taking advantage of favourable external factors, and securing support of the competent officials, etc., leading to the outstanding performance of their units. In the successful group too, the entrepreneurs had been able to change the course of their enterprises leading to significant improvement in the performance of their units by similar measures.

On the other hand, the units belonging to the average group had made only limited progress despite a good beginning because of the dependence on market conditions and the lack of required entrepreneurial initiations. In the sick group, the select units had become sick, despite good performance earlier, due to rejection of goods, non-realisation of bills, slump in demand, diversion of funds for working capital and neglect of business. The entrepreneur belonging to this group had not been able to change the course of their enterprises for better because of the lack of initiatives required on their part. However, one entrepreneur belonging to the average group who had introduced two new products (a perfumery extraction item and instant food items) after the slump in demand for his earlier product (Dehydrated Green Pepper) seemed to be promising. Similarly, one entrepreneur belonging to the sick group, who had to abondon the production of bungs for LPG cylinders, seemed to have taken the right kind of initiative.

10

REGIONAL VARIATIONS IN INDUSTRIAL CHARACTERISTICS AND PERFORMANCE

An attempt is made in this chapter to analyse variations in the industrial characteristics of the sample SSI units located in a developed region and backward regions. For this purpose, Bangalore District, which is a leading industrial district of the country and accounts for over 21 per cent of SSI units in the Karnataka State, has been classified as an industrially developed district. The other three sample districts, viz., Gulbarga, Dharwar and Mysore (GDM) have been classified as backward districts. These three districts together account for only about 20 per cent of the SSI units in Karnataka. While Gulbarga district accounts for only 3 per cent of SSI units in Karnataka, Dharwar and Mysore districts have been declared backward by the Government of India and both the districts are eligible for a central capital subsidy of 15 per cent. Thus, Bangalore district represents industrially developed region and other three districts represent industrially backward regions.

The industrial characteristics are being analysed in terms of product-type; average size of fixed investment, annual turnover, and employment; per employee fixed investment and annual turnover; and ratio of turnover to fixed investment.

Product-Type

In both the regions, engineering units, accounting for 50 per cent in Bangalore and 38 per cent in the other three districts, were dominant. The proportion of food and chemical units was greater in the backward region (14%) than in the developed region (10%). The same was true with regard to electrical and electronics units (22 per cent in backward regions and 16 per cent in developed regions). Thus, these three groups of industries together accounted for 76 per cent in the developed region and 74 per cent in the backward regions. Though, variation in the proportions of different types of industries across the regions was obvious, it was not found to be very significant except in the case of engineering group (Table 10.1).

TABLE 10.1: Percentage Distribution of the Sample SSI Units by Industrial-Product Type in Bangalore District and other Sample Districts

Industry Group	Bangalore	GDM*	Total
Food & Chemicals	9.7	13.8	11.7
Engineering	50.0	37.9	44.2
Electrical & Electronic	16.1	22.4	19.2
Leather, Rubber & Plastic	3.2	6.9	5.0
Paper, Printing & Packaging	3.3	5.2	4.1
Others (Unclassified)	17.7	13.8	15.8
Total	100.0	100.0	100.0
Number of Units	62	58	120

* Gulbarga, Dharwar & Mysore Districts

Average Size of Fixed Investment

Among the Industrial groups, average size of fixed investment was found to be the largest in the case of food and chemical group, followed by engineering group and paper, printing and packaging group. The fixed investment was found to be the smallest in the case of other (unclassified) groups (Table 10.2).

A comparison of average size of fixed investment in the different industrial groups across Bangalore and other three districts revealed that the average fixed investment, in 1987-88, was greater in Bangalore with regard to all the industrial groups, except electrical and electronics group, than that in other three districts. The regional variation in the size of fixed investment was found to be the most pronounced in the case of paper, printing and packaging group (226%), followed by the unclassified group (95%), leather, rubber and plastic group (89%), and food and chemical group (61%). As a whole, the average fixed investment was greater by 34 per cent in Bangalore than over that in the other three districts (Table 10.2).

TABLE 10.2: Average Fixed Investment (Rs. in 000) in the Year 1987-88 in Sample SSI Units

Industry Group	Bangalore	GDM	Total
Food & Chemicals	913.3	567.7	740.5
Engineering	691.4	592.1	651.3
Electrical & Electronics	546.5	546.8	546.7
Leather, Rubber & Plastic	787.5	417.8	541.0
Paper, Printing & Packaging	888.0	272.5	580.3
Others (Unclassified)	562.9	288.3	466.2
Total	693.6	516.1	605.3@

@ This figure would not tally with the same calculated performance-group wise because in the above table 9 units out of 120 units with extreme figures have not been taken into account. The same is true for the following tables in this chapter.

Average size of Annual Turnover

The averge size of turnover for the sample as a whole, in the year 1987-88, was found to be the largest in the food and chemical group (Rs. 16,44,200) and the smallest in the paper, printing and packaging group (Rs. 743,800). In Bangalore district, size of turnover was the largest in the engineering group (Rs. 15,13,300) and smallest in the paper, printing and packaging group (Rs. 750,000). In the other three districts, the average turnover was found to be the largest in the case of food and chemical group (Rs. 17,75,000) and the smallest in the case of other (unclassified) group (Rs. 513,000). As a whole, inter-industry group variation in the average annual turnover was found to be significant.

The regional variation in the size of average turnover was found to be the maximum in the engineering group where the size of turnover in Bangalore was greater by 87 per cent than that in other three districts. This was followed by the other (unclassified) group where the turnover in Bangalore was greater by 81 per cent than that in the other three districts. In the case of electrical and electronics group, and leather, rubber and plastic group, the turnovers were 59 per cent and 40 per cent respectively greater in the three backward districts than those in Bangalore district. The regional variation was found to be the least (2%) in the case of paper, printing and packaging group. However, as a whole the average size of sample SSI units, on the basis of annual turnover, was found to be larger in Bangalore (by 14%) than that in other three districts (Table 10.3).

TABLE 10.3: Average Turnover (Rs in 000) of Sample SSI units in the year 1987-88

Industry Group	Bangalore Dist.	GDM	Total
Food & Chemicals	1513.3	1775.0	1644.2
Engineering	1535.3	821.1	1246.9
Electrical & Electronics	1046.0	1661.4	1384.6
Leather, Rubber & Plastic	1240.0	1737.8	1571.8
Paper, Printing & Packaging	750.0	737.5	743.8
Others (unclassified)	930.2	513.0	782.9
Total	1316.4	1153.5	1243.0

Average Employment Size

For the sample as a whole, the average size of employment, in 1987-88, being 21 persons in the case of food and chemical group was found to be the largest one. This was followed by the unclassified group (18 persons) and engineering group (17 persons). The size of employment was found to be the smallest in the case of paper, printing and packaging group (13 persons). As for the regional variation in the average size of employment across the industrial groups, it was found to be the greatest in the case of paper, printing and packaging group as the average size of employment being 6 persons in the three districts was much smaller than the same being 20 persons in Bangalore district. The regional variation in the employment size was found to be quite significant in the case of engineering group as well as food and chemical group. As a whole, the size of average employment was greater in Bangalore district than those in the other three districts (Table 10.4).

Thus, the average size of sample SSI units, as indicated by the average size of fixed investment, annual turnover and employment, was found to be relatively larger in Bangalore district than that in the other three districts.

Per Employee Investment in Fixed Assets

The Per Employee Investment in Fixed Assets (PEIFA) was found to be the largest (Rs. 45,500) in the paper, printing and packaging group and the smallest in the case of unclassified group (Rs. 26,400). The inter-industry group variation in PEIFA in the case of other groups was found to be significant. As for the regional variation in PEIFA, the size of PEIFA was found to be larger in Bangalore district than that in other three districts in the case of all the industry groups except engineering group. In the engineering group, the PEIFA in Bangalore district was only Rs. 34,700 against Rs. 43,600 in the case of other three districts. Further, the regional variations in PEIFA across all the industrial groups were found to be significant. The overall regional variation in PEIFA indicated that the units located in Bangalore district were more capitial intestive than those in the other three districts. In other words, the units located in other three districts appeared to be more labour intensive than those in Bangalore district (Table 10.5).

TABLE 10.4: Average Size of Employment (in Persons) of Sample SSI units in the year 1987-88

Industry Group	Bangalore Dist.	GDM	Total
Food and Chemicals	18	23	21
Engineering	20	14	17
Electrical & Electronics	13	16	15
Leather, Rubber & Plastic	15	13	14
Paper, Printing & Packaging	20	6	13
Others (unclassified)	18	16	18
Total	18	15	17

TABLE 10.5: Per Employee Size of Fixed Investment (Rs in 000) in Sample SSI Units in the year 1987-88

Industry Group	Bangalore Dist.	GDM	Total
Food and Chemicals	49.8	24.9	36.0
Engineering	34.7	43.6	37.5
Electricals & Electronics	41.0	33.6	36.6
Leather, Rubber & Plastic	52.5	31.5	39.1
Paper, Printing & Packaging	45.5	45.4	45.5
Others (unclassified)	30.5	17.9	26.4
Total	37.8	33.8	37.0

Per Employee Size of Turnover

Per Employee Size of Turnover (PEST) was found to be the largest (Rs. 1,13,600) in the leather, rubber and plastic group and the smallest in the unclassified group (Rs. 44,300). This may suggest that the utilization of man-power was maximum in the leather, rubber and plastic group and minimum in the unclassified group. The variation in PEST was found to be significant across other industry groups as well. This meant that the extent of utilization of man-power varied significantly across the industrial groups.

The regional variation in PEST indicated that the utilization of man-power was better in Bangalore in the cases of food and chemical group, engineering group, and unclassified group than that in the other three districts. On the other hand, the man power utilization was found to be better in other three districts with regard to leather, rubber and plastic group, electrical and electronics group, and paper, printing and packaging group than that in Bangalore district. As a whole, the utilization of man power appeared to be better in the backward region comprising three sample districts than that in Bangalore district (Table 10.6).

TABLE 10.6: Per Employee Size of Turnover (Rs. in 000) in Sample SSI Units in the Year 1987-88

Industry Group	Bangalore Dist.	GDM	Total
Food and Chemicals	82.5	77.7	79.9
Engineering	77.0	60.5	71.8
Electrical & Electronics	78.5	102.1	92.6
Leather, Rubber & Plastic	82.7	131.2	113.6
Paper, Printing & Packaging	38.5	122.9	58.3
Others (unclassified)	50.4	31.7	44.3
Total	71.7	75.6	73.3

Ratio of Turnover to Fixed Investment

The Ratio of Turnover to Fixed Investment (RTF) was found to be the greatest (2.9) in leather, rubber and plastic group and the smallest (1.3) in paper, printing and packaging group. In other words, the utilization of fixed assets was found to be maximum in the leather, rubber and plastic group and minimum in the paper, printing and packaging group. As a whole, there was significant variation in the extent of utilization of fixed assets across the industrial groups. The second best utilization of fixed assets was found to be in the electrical and electronics group, followed by food and chemical group, engineering group, and unclassified group respectively.

As for the regional variation in RTF across the industry groups, RTF was found to be greater in other three districts (GDM) than that in Bangalore district with regard to all the industry groups except the engineering group. In the engineering group, RTF in Bangalore district being 2.2 was found to be substantially greater than that (1.4) in other three districts. While RTF was found to be substantially greater in the three districts than that in Bangalore district with regard to food and chemical group, electrical and electronics group, leather, rubber and plastic group, it was only marginally greater in the case of unclassified group. This might suggest that the utilization of fixed assets was better in the backward regions than that in a developed district, like Bangalore except in the case of engineering group. As a whole, the utilization of fixed assets was found to be better in the three backward districts than that in Bangalore district (Table 10.7).

TABLE 10.7: Ratio of Turnover to Fixed Investment of the Sample SSI Units in the Year 1987-88

Industry Group	Bangalore Dist.	GDM	Total
Food and Chemicals	1.7	3.1	2.2
Engineering	2.2	1.4	1.9
Electrical & Electronics	1.9	3.0	2.5
Leather, Rubber & Plastic	1.6	4.2	2.9
Paper, Printing & Packaging	0.8	2.7	1.3
Others (unclassified)	1.7	1.8	1.7
Total	1.9	2.2	3.0

Thus, the average size of investment on fixed assets, annual turnover and employment were found to be larger in Bangalore district than those in the other three districts (GDM) classified as backward. The capital intensity, as indicated by per employee fixed investment, was also found to be greater in Bangalore district than in the three backward districts. On the other hand, the utilization of man power, as indicated by per employee annual turnover, was found to be greater in the three backward districts than that in Bangalore district. Also, the utilization of fixed assets, appeared to be better in the three backward districts than that in Bangalore district. It may, therefore, be concluded that the promotion of industries in the backward area would not be disadvantageous in comparison to the same in a highly developed industrial and urban agglomeration.

Regional Variation in Performance of Sample SSI Units

It has already been discussed earlier in Chapter 1 that 15 per cent of the sample units were found to be very successful, 35 per cent successful, 32 per cent average and 18 per cent sick. As for the regional variation in the performance of sample units, 18 per cent of the sample units in Bangalore district were found to be very successful against only 12 per cent of those in the other three backward districts. While only 31 per cent of the sample units located in Bangalore district belonged to successful category, the proportion of units belonging to this category in the three backward districts was 39 per cent. Further, 35 per cent of the units in Bangalore district had average performance against only 28 per cent in the other three backward districts. As for the sick units, they accounted for 16 per cent in Bangalore district as against 21 per cent in the other three backward districts. Thus, the proportions of units having very successful performance and average performance were greater in the Bangalore district in comparison to other three districts. On the other hand, the proportions of successful units and sick units were greater in the backward districts in comparison to Bangalore district.

This may suggest that a highly developed industrial region can provide greater opportunity for outstanding performance of a SSI unit in comparison to an industrially backward region. Also, in a highly developed industrial region, a SSI unit even with unsatisfactory performance had a greater possibility to survive than in a backward region. On the other hand, if the performance of a SSI unit remain unsatisfactory for a longer period in an industrially backward region, there is a greater possibility of its becoming sick than its survival. Also, a SSI unit located in an industrially backward region can achieve reasonable success but the possibility of its becoming very successful (outstanding) would be rather limited in comparison to those located in an industrially developed region.

11

SUMMARY, CONCLUSIONS AND SUGGESTIONS

I. SUMMARY

1.1 The Sample

1.1.1 For the purpose of the study, a sample of 120 SSI units spread over four districts, viz., Bangalore, Mysore, Dharwar and Gulbarga of the Karnataka State was surveyed through a specially designed questionnaire. The sample SSI units were selected on the basis of size of investment in fixed assets, product-type, age of unit, and the background information on their present performance status. Out of 120 sample SSI units:

62 units were located in Bangalore;
30 units were located in Mysore District;
16 units were located in Dharwar District; and
12 units were located in Gulgarga District.

1.1.2 Eighty-one per cent of the sample units were more than five years old.
As for the distribution of sample units by the forms of organisation:

48 per cent of the units were proprietorship concerns;
39 per cent were partnership concerns;
12 per cent were private limited companies; and
one unit was a co-operative society.

1.1.3 As for the nature of activity:

63 per cent were engaged in manufacturing;
8 per cent in processing;
8 per cent in job-works;
2 per cent in servicing; and

the remaining units were engaged in a combination of activities.

1.1.4 Further, by product type:

44 per cent of the sample units were engineering units;
20 per cent were electrical and electronic units;
12 per cent were food and chemical units; and

the remaining units were producing or processing or servicing other items, like leather, rubber and plastic products, paper products, wooden and cement products etc.

1.1.5 The size of investment in plant and machinery in the year 1987-88, was:

Rs. 200,000 and below in 29 per cent of the sample units;
between Rs. 201,000 and Rs. 500,000 in 30 per cent of the units;
between Rs. 501,000 and Rs. 10,00,000 in 19 per cent of the units; and
above Rs. 10,00,000 in the remaining 22 per cent of the units.

1.2 Classification of Sample Units

1.2.1 For the purpose of analysis, the sample SSI units (except the sick units) were classified into three groups on the basis of selected performance indicators, viz.,

growth rate of investment in plant and machinery;
growth rate of employment;
growth rate of turnover;
growth rate of investment in plant and machinery per

employee;
growth rate of total productive capital per employee;
growth rate of turnover per employee;
ratio of turnover to investment in plant and machinery;
ratio of turnover to working capital; and
ratio of turnover to total productive capital.

The above mentioned growth rates of individual units were ranked and on the basis of the composite rank index for each unit, 98 sample units were classified into the following three groups:

very successful group (VSU) comprising 18 units;
successful group (SU) comprising 42 units; and
average group (AVU) comprising 38 units;

The remaining 22 sick units (SIKU) were treated as a separate group. Thus, all the 120 sample SSI units were classified into four performance-groups for analysis.

1.3 Profile of Units

1.3.1 It has already been mentioned earlier that 81 per cent of the sample SSI units were more than 5 years old. Such units accounted for 78 per cent in the very successful group, 76 per cent in the successful group, 84 per cent in the average group, and 86 per cent in the sick group. The average age for all the units worked out to 10.6 years. The same for the very successful group was 9.4 years, for the successful group 10.6 years, and for the average group and sick group 11 years. Thus, there was no significant difference in the age of sample units across the performance-groups. As such, the poor and unsatisfactory performance of the sample units belonging to the average group and sick group could not be attributed to their age.

1.3.2 The distribution of sample units by the form of organisation and performance-group revealed that proprietorship concern accounted for the largest proportion of the sample units in all the four performance-groups, followed by partnership concerns and private limited companies. However, the proprietorship units appeared to be more prone to sickness than the others.

1.3.3 The distribution of sample units by the size of fixed investment revealed that the average size of investment was the largest in the private limited companies (Rs. 11,59,800) and the smallest in the proprietorship units (Rs. 5,19,300).

1.3.4 Manufacturing was found to be the most dominant activity in all the four performance groups. Manufacturing as the sole activity was found to be significantly greater in the very successful group (78%), and successful group (64%) and sick group (59%).

1.3.5 Distribution of sample units by product type and performance-group revealed that the engineering units accounted for the greatest proportion of sample units in all the performance-groups, except sick group. In the sick group, the proportion of electrical and electronic units was the greatest.

1.3.6 The initial investment in plant and machinery did not exceed Rs. 500,000 in any of the units belonging to the very successful group. On the other hand, 26 per cent of the units belonging to the successful group, 18 per cent of those belonging to the average group, and 4 per cent of those belonging to the sick group had an initial investment of more than Rs. 500,000 on plant and machinery. The average initial fixed investment was the largest in the average group (Rs. 2,88,000) and the smallest in the very successful group (Rs. 1,61,300). This may lead to the conclusion that a large size of initial fixed investment is not necessary for the success of a SSI unit.

1.3.7 The distribution of sample units by the size of initial employment and the size of initial turnover also led to the same conclusion. The units with 10 or fewer employees in the initial year accounted for 58 per cent in the sick group and 90 per cent in the successful group. However, there was no significant variation in the average size of employment across the performance-groups, except the successful group. The average annual turnover in the initial year was found to be the smallest in the successful group (Rs. 147,900) and the largest in the average group (Rs. 4,28,838).

1.3.8 By the year 1987-88, significant changes had taken place in the size of fixed investment, employment, and turnover across the performance-groups on account of the differences in the performance levels.

The average size of fixed investment in the very successful group was the largest (Rs. 11,03,600) in the year 1987-88 against the same being smallest (Rs. 161,300) in the initial year.

In the case of successful group too, the average fixed investment had gone up from Rs. 262,600 in the initial year to Rs. 700,700 in the year 1987-88.

Against the above, the average fixed investment in the average group had gone up from Rs. 2,88,800 in the initial year to Rs. 4,15,300; and in the sick group from Rs. 167,500 to Rs. 3,11,300.

Thus, the quantum jumps in fixed assets in the successful and very successful groups were very noteworthy.

1.3.9 The average size of employment was the largest in the very successful group (34 persons) followed by the average group (17 persons), successful group (15 persons) and sick group (12 persons) against the same being 11,9,6 and 10 persons respectively in the initial year.

1.3.10 The average annual turnover was found to be the largest in the very successful group (Rs. 43,22,900), followed by the successful group (Rs. 13,07,600), average group (Rs. 12,39,400) and sick group (Rs. 3,85,600) against the same being Rs. 2,22,000, Rs. 1,47,900, Rs. 4,28,800 and Rs. 2,96,900 respectively in the initial year. This establishes a fairly strong link between volume of turnover and performance standard.

1.3.11 The average size for all the sample units during 1987-88, worked out to be:

investment – Rs. 5,99,700 against Rs. 2,36,700 in the initial year;

employment – 18 persons against 8 persons in the initial year; and

turnover – Rs. 15,92,600 against Rs. 2,73,500 in the initial year.

1.4. Profile of Sample Entrepreneurs

1.4.1 At the time of establishment of their units:

29 per cent of the entrepreneurs were 30 years of age or less;

51 per cent were in the age group of 31-40 years; and
20 per cent were more than 40 years old.

The average age of the sample entrepreneurs was found to be the highest in the sick group (39 years), followed by the very successful group (36 years), average group (35 years), and successful group (33 years). The average age for all the entrepreneurs was 35 years. There was a significant association between the age of entrepreneurs at the time of setting up of the units and their performance. Younger entrepreneurs seemed to have performed better.

1.4.2 About 22 per cent of the entrepreneurs were educated up to matriculation and below, 63 per cent were educated up to intermediate and graduation; and 15 per cent were post-graduates and other professional degree holders.

About 69 per cent of the entrepreneurs had received technical education and most of them had degree or diploma in engineering. The proportion of entrepreneurs with techincal education ranged between 61 per cent in the average group and 89 per cent in very successful group. However, no significant association between the level of education or technical education and performance-level was found.

1.4.3 The entrepreneurs who had received formal training accounted for 45 per cent of the sample entrepreneurs. Out of this 45 per cent, 24 per cent had received technical training, 12 per cent management training and 3 per cent had received entrepreneurship training. The proportion of entrepreneurs who had received training ranged between 41 per cent in the sick group and 50 per cent in the successful group.

1.4.4 Eighty-two per cent of the sample entrepreneurs had previous work experience before they set up their units. The proportion of such entrepreneurs ranged between 79 per cent in the case of successful group and 91 per cent in the case of sick group.

1.4.5 The combined share of entrepreneurs whose immediate previous occupations were in industries and trade related activities, like production, marketing, general management, ownership or partnership was the greatest in the sick group (82%), followed by the average group (64%), successful group

(50%), and very successful group (39%). Thus, mere relevant experience did not seem to be adequate enough to ensure the success of a SSI entrepreneur.

1.4.6 The average annual income (from all sources) of the sample entrepreneurs before they set up their units was worked out to be Rs. 33,900. The average annual income was found to be the largest in the very successful group (Rs. 68,100), followed by the successful group (Rs. 31,200), average group (Rs. 26,000), and sick group (Rs. 24,800). There was significant association between the size of annual income and the performance level. The entrepreneurs with better economic status seemed to have performed better.

1.4.7 No significant association between the educational level of entrepreneurs' fathers or guardians and the performance of sample entrepreneurs was found. However, there seemed to be a significant association between the occupations of entrepreneurs fathers or guardians and entrepreneurs' performance. The proportion of entrepreneurs whose fathers or guardians' occupation was agriculture was greatest in the sick group (40%) and the smallest in the very successful group (7%). On the other hand, the entrepreneurs whose fathers or guardians' occupation was business or service in the private firms was the greatest in the very successful group (71%) and the smallest in the sick group (15%).

1.5 Motivation

1.5.1 The factors that motivated the sample entrepreneurs to set up SSI units were analysed in terms of ambition, compulsion, encouragement, consideration and expectation. Among the ambition-factors:

desire to be self-employed was found to be the most important factor, followed by
the desire to make economic gains,
desire to prove one's capability,
desire to gain social prestige, and
other factors, like the desire to develop an import-substitution item, to introduce something new in the market, and to secure a better future for children, etc.

The relative importance of the first three most important motivating-factors was the same across all the four performance-groups. It was found that most of the entrepreneurs were motivated by their own desire to set up SSI units rather than by the desire of their parents and other relatives.

1.5.2 Among the compulsion-factors, dissatisfaction with the previous job or occupation was found to be the most compelling-factor for motivating the entrepreneurs to set up their SSI units across all the four performance groups. The diversification of economic interests was the second most compelling-factor except in the sick group. While unemployment was found to be the second most compelling-factor in the sick group, it was not at all reported in the very successful group and it was of the least importance in the successful group. This would perhaps mean that a good proportion of entrepreneurs belonging to the sick group would have been hard-pressed to get into something and they would not have been able to spend sufficient time in considering the pros and cons of setting up of their units.

1.5.3 Among the encouraging-factors, previous experience was found to be the most encouraging-factor, followed by the success stories of other entrepreneurs, acquired professional or technical skills, and encouragement from the family members and relatives. The least encouraging-factor was found to be the acquired or inherited property. Thus, the sample entrepreneurs got greater confidence from their own abilities and skills than from the financial and material resources available to them. The success-stories of other entrepreneurs being the second-most encouraging factor indicated that the success of an entrepreneur could have a multiplier-effect on the generation of entrepreneurship. The encouragement from family and relatives being the first most encouraging-factor in the very successful group and fourth most important factor in the other groups indicated that the moral and material support from the families and relatives would have been forthcoming with greater ease to the entrepreneurs belonging to the very successful group than to those belonging to the other groups. This would have enabled the entrepreneurs belonging to the very successful group to enter into entrepreneurship with greater confidence which might have enhanced their propensity to take risks.

1.5.4 Previous employment in industries or trades was found to be the most important consideration for the selection of products by the sample entrepreneurs. This was followed by the easy process of setting up a unit, easy availability of technical know-how, easy availability of machinery, and lack of competition. Other considerations that did not leave any choice to entrepreneurs in the selection of products, such as allotment of product-item by parent units, and prior commitment (to self) for producing a particular item, were ranked sixth. The presence of such entrepreneurs who had selected their products without any rational consideration was found to be the most conspicuous in the sick group. These entrepreneurs had run into trouble because they had not taken into account the limitation of their own resources, inadequacies of the existing support-systems, and the commercial implications of borrowed capital. Though the difference in the relative importance of factors considered across the performance-groups was significant, no definite pattern emerged.

1.5.5 The sample entrepreneurs had very high expectations of getting industrial accommodation and financial resources from the institutional sources, followed by the availability of financial supports from their own families and relatives. On the other hand, they had very low expectations of getting technical assistance and assistance in the marketing of products, and in the supply of machinery and raw materials from the institutional sources.

1.6 Support Received in Setting up the Unit

1.6.1 While expectation can be helpful in the stimulation of entrepreneurship, the formation and consolidation of entrepreneurship would depend on the extent of fulfilment of expectation. An analysis of the fulfilment of sample entrepreneurs' expectations revealed that the extent of fulfilment was reasonably good. The overall extent of complete fulfilment was worked out to be 62 per cent. It was found to be greater in the average group (75%) and sick group (65%) than in the very successful group (63%) and successful group (52%).

The assistance from the institutional sources with regard to technical know-how, marketing of products and the supply of machinery and raw materials was not only the least expected by the entrepreneurs, but also the least fulfilled. As such, these could be considered to be the weak areas of existing promotional support-systems.

1.6.2 About 38 per cent of the sample entrepreneurs had not faced any major problem that might have discouraged them in the process of setting up of their units. The proportion of such entrepreneurs was the greatest in the average group (60%), followed by the very successful group (33%), sick group (32%), and successful group (24%). The analysis of information furnished by the remaining 62 per cent of the sample entrepreneurs revealed that:

the shortage of working capital was the most discouraging factor, followed by;
the delay in power connection;
inadequacy of finance for acquiring fixed assets; and
delay in the allotment of plot or shed in the industrial estates.

1.6.3 About 60 per cent of the sample entrepreneurs were reported to have faced various problems in obtaining techno-economic information, infrastructural facilities, and financial assistance, etc. As a whole, the major problems reported were:

undue delay in sanction and approval;
complicated procedures; and
lack of knowledge and necessary competency on the part of concerned officials.

1.6.4 About 88 per cent of pre-operative expenses incurred by the sample entrepreneurs were met from their own funds and the remaining 12 per cent were met from the funds provided by their families. The proportion of funds for pre-operative expenses provided by the entrepreneurs' families was found to be the greatest in the very successful group (15%) and the smallest in the sick group (3%).

1.6.5 For the initial fixed investment on plant and machinery by the entrepreneurs:

37 per cent of the required funds had been provided by the KSFC;
25 per cent by the public sector banks; and
4 per cent by NSIC and KSSIDC together.

Thus, 67 per cent of the funds required for initial fixed investment had come from the public sector institutional sources.

The entrepreneurs' own contribution to the initial fixed investment was worked out to be 31 per cent; and the remaining 2 per cent of the required funds had come from private banks and other sources.

The proportion of funds from the institutional sources ranged between 63 per cent (in the average group) and 72 per cent (in the sick group). Entrepreneurs' own contributions ranged between 25 per cent (in the sick group) and 35 per cent (in the average group).

1.6.6 As for the initial working capital, entrepreneurs' own contribution was 17 per cent and that of commercial banks was 77 per cent. The entrepreneurs own contribution was found to be the smallest in the sick group (14%) and the greatest in the average group (23%). The contribution of commercial banks was the smallest in the verv successful group (68%) and the greatest in the sick group (81%). As a whole entreprenerus belonging to the sick group had received greater institutional support for meeting their requirements of initial fixed investment as well as working capital than those belonging to the very successful group.

1.6.7 It was found in the year 1987-88, the contribution of institutional sources to the funds for fixed investment was 64 per cent and that of the entrepreneurs was 32 per cent. Thus, no significant change had taken place in the shares of these two sources in the year 1987-88 over those in the initial year. However, it was observed that the contribution of KSFC had come down marginally from 37 per cent in the initial year to 34 per cent in 1987-88, and that of the public sector commercial banks had gone up from 25 per cent to 30 per cent. Further, there were significant differences in the contributions of individual sources, like KSFC, banks and others with regard to individual performance-groups in 1987-88 over those in the initial years. The contribution of other sources in the sick group had gone up from 3 per cent in the initial year to 11 per cent in the year 1987-88.

1.6.8 The contribution of entrepreneurs in the working capital had come down from 17 per cent in the initial year to 15 per cent in the year 1987-88, and that of the public sector commercial banks had gone up from 72 per cent to 76 per cent. While there was a significant increase in the contribution of public sector commercial banks in the very successful group (from 54% to 78%), there was a significant increase in the entrepreneurs own contribution in the sick group (from 14% to 21%) possibly because of the discontinuation of working capital facility by banks in some cases.

1.6.9 A comparison of financial support for fixed investment provided by KSFC and the public sector commercial banks revealed that in the initial year while 59 per cent of assistance from KSFC had gone to the successful group, 67 per cent of assistance from the banks had gone to the average group. In the year 1987-88, the very successful group and successful group together accounted for 75 per cent of the assistance provided by KSFC and 55 per cent the assistance provided by banks. The average size of financial assistance from KSFC was much larger than that from banks in the initial year as well as in the year 1987-88.

1.7 Operational Problems

1.7.1 Before identifying the operational problems, the extent of availability of different inputs, infrastructural facilities and demand for products to the sample SSI units were examined. As a whole the extent of availability of inputs, etc., to the requirement in the initial year was found to be 91 per cent. The extent of availability was found to be greater in the average and sick groups than that in the very successful and successful groups.

The availability of funds for investment in fixed assets ranged between 91 per cent in the very successful group and 97 per cent in the sick group.

The availability of funds for working capital ranged

between 80 per cent in the successful group and 87 per cent in the average group.

The advantage of demand for products ranged between 75 per cent in the successful group and 82 per cent in the sick group.

Thus, the units belonging to the average and sick groups did not have any major disadvantage in comparison to those belonging to the very successful and successful groups to begin with so far as the availability of inputs, facilities and demand for products were concerned.

During the period 1985-88, the overall extent of availability to the requirement was found to be almost the same as in the initial year. However, some significant differences were found with regard to the availability of individual factors across the performance-groups during the period 1985-88 over that in the initial year. The availability of working capital in the case of sick group had declined from 81 per cent in the initial year to 61 per cent during the period 1985-88. Similarly, the demand for products in the sick group had declined from 81 per cent to 69 per cent while the same had gone up from 74 per cent to 91 per cent in the case of successful group.

1.7.2 Among the major operational problems faced by the sample entrepreneurs in the initial year:

marketing problems were found to be the most difficult ones, followed by
the shortage of working capital;
labour problems;
inadequacy of capital for fixed investment;
power supply problem; and
problems in the supply of raw materials.

Marketing problems and the shortage of working capital were found to be the two most important problems across all the performance-groups in the initial year. As a whole, no definite pattern in the operational problems faced by the sample entrepreneurs across the performance-groups in the initial year was found.

1.7.3 During the period 1985-88, the shortage of working capital was found to be the most difficult problem, followed by labour problems, marketing problems, and power supply problems. While the problems on account of marketing and inadequacy of capital for investment in fixed assets had become less acute, the same on account of the shortage of working capital, power supply, labour, and government policies had become relatively more acute. A comparison of the relative importance of major problems across the performance-groups did not reveal any clear-cut pattern.

1.7.4 Among the problems related to raw materials in the initial year, the scarcity of raw materials was found to be the most difficult problem followed by the high cost of raw materials. During the period 1985-88, the high cost of raw materials was found to be the most difficult problem, followed by the scarcity of raw materials, and poor quality of raw materials.

1.7.5 Among the problems related to power supply, inadequacy was found to be the most difficult problem, followed by uncertainty, and high cost in the initial year. The relative importance of these problems continued to be the same during the period 1985-88. As a whole, the sample entrepreneurs were not so much concerned about the high cost, but were very concerned about the inadequacy and uncertainty of power supply.

1.7.6 As for the nature of marketing problems faced in the initial year, the problems, like inadequate and irregular order from the parent units, lack of ISI mark and stiff competition due to imports, etc., were found to be the most difficult problems. These were followed by the demand for credit, and competition from the other SSI units.

While the issue of greatest concern of the very successful units was competition with other SSI units; and for the successful units it was marketing of products on credit basis; the greatest concern of the average and sick units was of not getting adequate orders from the large scale units.

During the period 1985-88, demand on credit was found to be the most difficult problem, followed by the competition from SSI units, and slackness in demand. The demand on credit was found to be the second most difficult problem in all the four performance-groups. While marketing of products on credit-basis is not an unusual marketing practice, the main problem was the inordinate delay in the realisation of bills which resulted in the shortage of working capital on the one hand and enhancement of the cost of capital on the other.

1.7.7 Among the major manpower problems in the initial year, lack of skilled workers was found to be the most difficult problem, followed by job-hopping by workers, and absenteeism. Trade unionism was found to be the least difficult problem.

During the period 1985-88, the relative importance of different labour problems remained almost in the same order as in the initial year.

1.7.8 Only one-fourth of the sample entrepreneurs felt that the labour laws posed a serious problem. The provision of ESI was found to be the most difficult problem in the initial year. On the other hand, during the period 1985-88, the minimum wage/salary was found to be the most difficult problem, followed by the ESI. The main problem on account of Factories Act was reported that once a unit came under the Act, it had to extend all the welfare measures to its workers even when its performance was not upto the mark or it was sick. The main problem with regard to the provision of ESI was its misuse by workers.

1.7.9 Only about 14 per cent of the sample entrepreneurs came forward to furnish information on the management problems of their enterprises. In the initial year:

production management was found to be the most difficult problem; followed by problems in
financial management;
labour management; and
marketing management.

During the period 1985-88, production management and financial management continued to be the first and second most important problems, followed by marketing management and labour management. In the sick group, only marketing management was reported to be the problem area.

1.7.10 Among the individual government policies and rules, the provision of sales tax was found to be the most difficult problem in the initial year. This was followed by the provisions of excise duty and income tax. During the period 1985-88, the provision of excise duty was found to be the most problematic one, followed by that of sales tax, and income tax. According to the sample entrepreneurs, the main problem was not the rate of excise duty but the complicated procedure involved and the required detailed documentation. Even a minor error in the procedure or documentation often led to harassment by the concerned officials. The same was true with regard to the sales tax. Further, the sample entrepreneurs opined that there should be uniform rates of sales tax all over the country as the inter-state differences in the rates of sales tax created problems for the marketing of products not only outside the state but also within a state. A few of the sample entrepreneurs felt that some of the statutory obligations were problems for them.

1.7.11 Some of the serious problems (that had left a lasting impact) faced by some of the sample units during the first four years, those during the fifth year to the ninth year, and after ninth year since their establishment were analysed. The analysis revealed that the units belonging to very successful group and successful group too had faced almost similar problems as faced by the units belonging to the average and sick groups. As such, the better performance of very successful group and successful group could not be attributed to the absence of problems; nor poor or unsatisfactory performance of the units belonging to the average and sick groups could be attributed only to the serious problems faced by them. An analysis of the efforts made by the sample entrepreneurs to overcome the serious problems faced by them revealed that it was relatively easier to overcome production problems and labour problems than marketing problems and financial problems. Overcoming of the financial problems appeared to be the most difficult one for most of the units.

1.8 Performance

1.8.1 The average annual growth rate of fixed investment for all the sample units worked out to 9 per cent. It was found to be the lowest in the average group (3%) and highest in the very successful group (23%).

The annual growth rate of working capital for the sample as whole was 12 per cent and it ranged between 25 per cent in the very successful group and minus one per cent in the sick group.

The annual growth rate of total productive capital (fixed and working) was 10 per cent for the sample as a whole and it ranged between 24 per cent in the very successful group and 2 per cent in the sick group.

The annual growth rate of turnover for all the sample units was found to be 19 per cent. It was lowest in the sick group (13%) and highest in the very successful group (38%).

The annual growth rate of employment for all the sample units was worked out to be 7 per cent. The same was found to be the lowest in the sick group (2%) and highest in the very successful group (13%).

Thus, the annual growth rates of all the five indices were highest in the very successful group, followed by the successful group, average group and sick group except that the growth rate of fixed capital was greater in the sick group (6%) than that in the average group (3%).

1.8.2 The per employee fixed capital in 1987-88 over that in the initial year had increased by 105 per cent in the very successful group and 55 per cent in the sick group. The same had declined by 3 per cent in the successful group and by 9 per cent in the average group. It had increased by 21 per cent for the total sample units. The annual growth rate was found to be 2 per cent for the sample as a whole. It ranged between 8 per cent in the very successful group and minus one per cent in the average group.

The per employee working capital for the total sample units during the same period had increased by 52 per cent. It was the highest in the very successful group (137%), followed by the successful group (84%), and average group (42%). The same had declined by 26 per cent in the case of sick group. The annual growth rate was 4 per cent for the total sample and it ranged between 10 per cent in the very successful group and minus 3 per cent in the sick group.

The increase in the per employee total productive capital for the sample as a whole was 31 per cent. It was highest in the very successful group (118%) and lowest in the average group (3%). The annual growth rate was 3 per cent for the total sample and the same ranged between 9 per cent in the very successful group and 0.2 per cent in the average group.

The increase in the per employee annual turnover for the total sample, during the same period, was found to be 201 per cent. It was found to be highest in the very successful group

(506%) and lowest in the sick group (19%). The annual growth rate was found to be 11 per cent for the total sample, and it ranged between 12 per cent in the very successful group and 2 per cent in the sick group.

1.8.3 The ratio of the working capital to fixed capital for the total sample had increased from 0.5 in the initial year to 0.7 in the year 1987-88. The same had increased from 0.8 to 0.9 in the very successful group, from 0.3 to 0.6 in the successful group and from 0.4 to 0.6 in the average group. It had declined from 1.5 to 0.7 in the sick group. Thus, the financial structure of the sample units was the most balanced in the case of very successful group.

The ratio of turnover to fixed capital for the total sample had increased from 1.0 in the initial year to 2.5 in the year 1987-88. The same had increased from 1.4 to 4.5 in the very successful group, from 0.5 to 1.9 in the successful group, and from 1.1 to 1.9 in the average group. It had declined from 1.6 to 1.3 in the sick group. Thus, the utilization of fixed capital was most efficient in the very successful group. While it had declined in the sick group, other three groups had experienced significant improvement.

The ratio of turnover to the working capital had increased from 1.8 in the initial year to 3.6 in the year 1987-88. The same had increased from 1.8 to 3.9 in the very successful group, from 1.9 to 3.4 in the successful group, from 2.9 to 3.4 in the average group and from 1.1 to 1.8 in the sick group. Thus, the utilization of working capital was most efficient in the very successful group, and the improvement in the efficiency was the least in the average group followed by the sick group.

The ratio of turnover to total productive capital for the sample as a whole had gone up from 0.6 in the initial year to 1.5 in the year 1987-88. The same had increased from 0.8 to 2.1 in the very successful group, 0.4 to 1.2 in the successful group, from 0.8 to 1.2 in the average group and from 0.7 to 0.8 in the sick group. Thus, the utilization of total productive capital was most efficient in the very successful group and least efficient in the sick group. Improvement in efficiency of utilization was maximum in the successful group and minimum in the sick group.

1.8.4 The analysis of capital borrowed for fixed investment and the outstanding against the same till the year 1987-88, revealed that the repayment behaviour of the very successful and successful entrepreneurs was much better than that of those belonging to the average group and sick group. The net increase in the capital borrowed for fixed investment till the year 1987-88 over the capital borrowed fixed investment in the initial year was 620 per cent in the very successful group. Against this net addition of capital borrowed for fixed investment over that in the initial year, the percentage of outstanding capital borrowed for fixed investment to the total capital borrowed for fixed investment in the year 1987-88 was 27 per cent in the very successful group, 23 per cent in the successful group, 39 per cent in the average group and 137 per cent in the sick group. Thus, the outstanding amount in the sick group was more than the principal amount because of accumulated interest amount.

1.8.5 The ability of the entrepreneur and his immediate environment were found to be the first set of most important factors responsible for the performance of entrepreneurs belonging to the very successful group and the successful group. While there was a great deal of similarity between the two groups with regard to the relative importance of factors responsible for their performance, there were some significant differences as well. The very successful entrepreneurs seemed to be attaching greater importance to sustaining and improving the quality of their products and maintaining production schedules while the successful entrepreneurs seemed to have greater dependence on demand for their products and marketing strategies adopted by them. Similarly, while the very successful entrepreneurs appeared to be attaching a lot of importance to maintaining good relationship with their customers and suppliers, the successful entrepreneurs did not give that much importance to this factor.

In the average group, the performance of sample units was attributed to a combination of favourable factors and unfavourable factors. These entrepreneurs seemed to have greater dependence on the quality of their products and demand for the same than on their entrepreneurial abilities to intervene into the environment in order to carve out a niche for themselves. In the sick group, the reported shortage of working capital was found to be the most important factor for their poor performance. This was followed by marketing problems, inadequate and untimely support from the government agencies, and production problems.

1.9 Desire for Growth to the Level of Medium Scale Unit

1.9.1 About 28 per cent of the sample entrepreneurs were willing to allow their units to become medium scale units. The proportion of entrepreneurs favouring their units to grow to the level of medium scale was greater in the better performing groups.

1.9.2 The major advantages that such entrepreneurs foresaw were:

possibility of reducing the cost of production, and easy expansion, diversification and modifications of their units;
possibility of reducing the marketing cost and diversification of market; and
others, like greater bargaining power, greater export possibilities, greater benefit on tax, etc.

The entrepreneurs who were not intending to allow their units to become medium scale units felt that there was a greater advantage in remaining as small scale units. The other reasons reported were unfavourable government policy and complicated procedures, limited managerial capacity of entrepreneurs, and the possibility of labour problems, etc.

1.10 Future Plan for Unit

1.10.1 About 59 per cent of the sample entrepreneurs had some form of future plans for the growth of their units.

1.10.2 Among these, plan for product-diversification was found to be the most common followed by the expansion of unit, expansion and diversification of market, modernisation of unit, and so on.

1.10.3 Among the sick group, plan for rehabilitation was the most important one, followed by securing sub-contract or ancillary relationship.

1.11 Sickness and Rehabilitation

1.11.1 Analysis of sickness among the sample units revealed that a unit may become sick at any point of time during its life-span. In about 90 per cent of the cases, the symptoms of sickness were noticed by the entrepreneurs on their own. Mounting liabilities, and shrinking working capital were found to be major symptoms of sickness.

1.11.2 Though most of the entrepreneurs had taken a variety of initiatives for preventing sickness of their units, none of them had been able to prevent sickness of his unit. Out of the 22 units in the sick group, only 14 had been declared sick and the viability studies had been completed in the case of 10 units. According to the viability studies, as reported by the concerned entrepreneurs, all the 10 units had been found viable and eligible for rehabilitation.

1.11.3 Out of the 10 units for which viability studies had been conducted, only 4 units were under the so-called rehabilitation programme during the study period. However, the rehabilitation process of sick units did not seem to be systematic. No systematic efforts had been made to diagnose the causes of sickness. The rehabilitation package also did not seem to be a comprehensive one. Only two units appeared to have been under some sort of rehabilitation programme.

1.11.4 An analysis of the select cases of sickness since inception revealed that the sickness had set in at the initial stage itself in a few of the sample units due to the lop-sided emphasis on some aspects or neglect of one or more key aspects in planning and management of the enterprise.

1.12 Turning Points: Cases of Select Sample Units

1.12.1 Analysis of turning points in the select cases of sample units across the four performance-groups revealed that the performance of an enterprise neither follows the same direction nor moves at the same pace for ever. Some of the sample units that could be classified as very successful and successful had faced teething problems and were at the verge of demise once upon a time. Similarly, some of the units that were found to be sick or whose performance was not upto the expectation were flourishing once upon a time. Thus, the failure of an entrepreneur at one point of time does not mean that he is doomed for ever. Similarly, an entrepreneur successful at one point of time need not remain successful for ever if he does not keep himself abreast with the changing business environment and prepared for the inevitable in future.

1.12.2 It is obvious that the performance of a SSI unit very much depends on the quality of entrepreneurship. The select units belonging to the very successful group had faced the problems of limited demand, rejection of goods, poor performance, financial constraints, stiff competition, etc., but the entrepreneurs could change the course of their units leading to outstanding performance by:

changing and diversifying product range;
improving quality of products;
deploying own resources;
taking advantage of external factors; and
changing business strategies.

Almost the same was true in the case of select sample units belonging to the successful group.

In the case of average group, the select sample units had made only limited progress despite a good beginning because of the dependence on market situations and lack of required entrepreneurial initiatives. In the case of sick group, the select sample units were languishing, despite good performance earlier because of rejection of goods, non-realisation of bills, slump in demand, diversion of funds, and neglect of business by the entrepreneurs.

1.13.1 The average size of investment on fixed assets annual turnover and employment were found to be larger in Bangalore district than those in other three districts GDM (Gulbarga, Dharwar and Mysore together) classified as backward.

1.13.2 The sample SSI units located in Bangalore district were found to be more capital intensive than those located in other three backward districts.

1.13.3 The utilization of man power and fixed assets appeared to be better in the three backward districts than that in Bangalore district.

1.13.4 While Bangalore district accounted for larger proportions of very successful units and average units, the three backward districts accounted for larger proportions of successful units and sick units.

II. CONCLUSIONS

2.1 Analysis of profiles of sample SSI units revealed that

2.1.1 Proprietorship concerns were more prone to sickness than the partnership concerns and private limited companies (1.3.2);*

2.1.2 Manufacturing, as the sole activity, was more prominent in the very successful and successful groups than in the average and sick groups (1.3.4);

2.1.3 The sample units producing electrical and electronic items were found to be more prone to sickness than others (1.3.5); and

2.1.4 The small size of a SSI unit in the initial stage was not a limiting factor for the growth and outstanding performance in future and, therefore, a SSI entrepreneur should not be unduly concerned about the small size of his unit at the initial stage (1.3.6 to 1.3.10).

2.2 Analysis of sample entrepreneurs' background profiles revealed that

2.2.1 At the time of setting up of sample units, the better performing entrepreneurs were relatively young and the ideal age group for starting a SSI enterprise appeared to be 31 to 40 years (1.4.1);

2.2.2 The educational level, technical qualifications, formal training and previous work experience of entrepreneurs were not found to be significantly associated with the performance levels of their units (1.4.2 to 1.4.5);

2.2.3 The entrepreneurs with better economic status before the setting up of their units seemed to have performed better (1.4.6); and

2.2.4 The entrepreneurs coming from business families seemed to have performed better than those coming from the families of agriculturists (1.4.7).

2.3 Analysis of motivating factors revealed that

2.3.1 The desire to be self-employed was the greatest motivating factors to become SSI entrepreneurs (1.5.1);

2.3.2 entrepreneurs were motivated by their own ambitions rather

* Numbers in parenthesis refer to the paras in the summary section in this chapter.

than the ambitions of their parents' and other relatives (1.5.1);

2.3.3 dissatisfaction with previous job or occupation was the most compelling factor for the entrepreneurs to enter into industry (1.5.2);

2.3.4 while the diversification of the economic interests was the second most compelling factor for the entrepreneurs belonging to the very successful, successful and average groups, unemployment was the second most compelling factor for the entrepreneurs belonging to the sick group motivating them to enter into industry (1.5.2);

2.3.5 the greatest source of encouragement for the sample as a whole was previous experience, but in the case of very successful group, encouragement from the family and relatives was the most important one (1.5.3);

2.3.6 the entrepreneurs got greater confidence from their own abilities and skills than from financial and other material resources available to them (1.5.3);

2.3.7 previous employment in industry or trade was found to be the most important consideration for the selection of products for the sample as a whole, but in the case of sick group, lack of choice in the selection of products was found to be the most important one (1.5.4); and

2.3.8 accommodation in an industrial estate and the availability of financial resources from institutional sources were the greatest expectations of entrepreneurs (1.5.5).

2.4 Analysis of support for setting up SSI units received by the sample entrepreneurs revealed that

2.4.1 extent of total fulfilment of expectations was reasonably good (1.6.1);

2.4.2 extent of total fulfilment of expectations was greater in the average and sick groups than that in the very successful and successful groups (1.6.1);

2.4.3 the assistance from the institutional sources in marketing of products and the supply of technical know-how, machinery and raw materials were the weak areas of existing promotional support-system (1.6.1);

2.4.4 shortage of working capital was the most discouraging factor followed by the delay in power connections, inadequate funds for fixed investments, and the delay in allotment of plot or shed in an industrial estate (1.6.2);

2.4.5 major problems faced in getting the various facilities and financial support were undue delay, complicated procedures and the lack of required knowledge and competency on the part of concerned officials (1.6.3);

2.4.6 the sample entrepreneurs had met most of the pre-operative expenses from their own funds (1.6.4);

2.4.7 about two-thirds of funds required for fixed investments had come from institutional sources (1.6.5 and 1.6.7);

2.4.8 about three-fourths of the working capital requirement had been provided by banks (1.6.6 and 1.6.8);

2.4.9 the entrepreneurs belonging to the sick group had received greater financial support in the initial stage than those belonging to the very successful group (1.6.6); and

2.4.10 the average size of financial assistance for fixed investment provided by KSFC was much larger than that provided by the commercial banks (1.6.9).

2.5 Analysis of the operational problems revealed that

2.5.1 the extent of availability of required inputs, facilities and demand for products in the initial year was good, and it was greater in the average and sick groups than that in the very successful group (1.7.1);

2.5.2 the units belonging to the average and sick groups did not have any major disadvantage in comparison to those belonging to the very successful and successful groups at the initial stage, though the availability of the working capital and demand for products had declined significantly in the case of the sick group during the period 1985-88 (1.7.1);

2.5.3 major operational problem faced by the sample units in the initial year were marketing problems, followed by shortage of working capital, labour problems, inadequacy of capital for fixed investment and power supply problem (1.7.2);

2.5.4 during the period 1985-88, shortage of working capital was the most difficult problem, followed by labour problem, marketing problem and power supply problem (1.7.3);

2.5.5 high cost and scarcity were the major raw material problems faced (1.7.4);

2.5.6 inadequacy and uncertainty were the major power supply problems (1.7.5);

2.5.7 demand on credit and competition from other SSI units were the major marketing problems (1.7.6);

2.5.8 lack of skilled workers, absenteeism and job-hopping were the major man power problems (1.7.7);

2.5.9 the provisions of ESI and minimum wage/salary were the major labour law problems and the main complaint against the ESI was its misuse by workers (1.7.8);

2.5.10 production, finance, marketing and labour were the major management problem areas (1.7.9);

2.5.11 the entrepreneurs were not so much concerned about the rates of excise duties and sales tax as about the complicated procedure and detailed documentations required (1.7.10);

2.5.12 the better performance of very successful group was not because of the absence of serious problems since they too had faced almost similar problems as faced by the entrepreneurs belonging to te other two groups (1.7.11); and

2.5.13 it was easier for the entrepreneurs to overcome production problems and labour problems than financial problems and marketing problems faced by them (1.7.11).

2.6 Analysis of the performance of sample units revealed that

2.6.1 the group of sample units performing better had experienced higher rates of growth in capital, employment and turnover (1.8.1);

2.6.2 the performance of very successful group was outstanding with regard to the growth in capital as well as turnover per employee (1.8.2);

2.6.3 the performance of successful group was impressive with regard to growth in turnover per employee but modest with regard to growth in capital per employee (1.8.2);

2.6.4 the performance of average group was modest with regard to growth in turnover per employee, but insignificant with regard to growth in capital per employee (1.8.2);

2.6.5 the performance of sick group was low with regard to growth in turnover as well as capital per employee (1.8.2);

2.6.6 the financial structure was found to be the most balanced in the very successful group (1.8.3);

2.6.7 the utilization of capital had improved significantly in the very successful group and successful group, modest in the average group, and almost stagnant in the sick group (1.8.3);

2.6.8 the utilization of capital was more efficient in the better performing group (1.8.3); and

2.6.9 the repayment behaviour of the entrepreneurs belonging to the very successful group and the successful group was much better than that of those belonging to the average group and sick group (1.8.4).

2.7 Analysis of factors responsible for the performance of sample units, as reported by the sample entrepreneurs, revealed that

2.7.1 ability and immediate environment of the entrepreneurs belonging to the very successful group and successful group were the main factors responsible for very good and reasonably good performances of their units respectively (1.8.5);

2.7.2 rather unsatisfactory performance of the entrepreneurs belonging to the average group was because of their greater dependence on the market situations than on their own abilities (1.8.5); and

2.7.3 poor performance of the units belonging to the sick group was mainly due to the unsatisfactory entrepreneurial efforts, shortage of working capital, marketing problems, and production problems (1.8.5).

2.8 Analysis of willingness of entrepreneurs to allow their units to grow to become a medium scale unit revealed that

2.8.1 the willingness of entrepreneurs to allow their units become medium scale units was greater in the better performing groups (1.9.1);

2.8.2 major advantages of a medium scale unit were the possibility of reduction in the cost of production and marketing, and expansion and diversification of product-range and market (1.9.2); and

2.8.3 major reasons for unwillingness were the advantages of remaining a SSI unit, unfavourable government policies and complicated procedures, limited managerial capacity of entrepreneurs, and the possibility of labour problems (1.9.3).

2.9 Analysis of plans of the sample entrepreneurs to be implemented in the near-future revealed that

2.9.1 more than one-half of the sample entrepreneurs had some form of future plans for the growth of their units (1.10.1);

2.9.2 plan for product diversification was the largest, followed by expansion of unit, expansion and diversification of market, and modernisation of unit (1.10.2); and

2.9.3 plan for rehabilitation was the most important one in the sick group (1.10.3).

2.10 Analysis of sickness among the sample units revealed that

2.10.1 a SSI unit may become sick at any point of time during its life-span (1.11.1);

2.10.2 most of the entrepreneurs belonging to the sick group had noticed the symptoms of sickness of their units on their own (1.11.1);

2.10.3 mounting liabilities and shrinking working capital were the major symptoms of sicnkess (1.11.1);

2.10.4 though most of the entrepreneurs belonging to the sick group had taken preventive measures, none really had succeeded in preventing the sickness of his unit (1.11.2);

2.10.5 no systematic approach seemed to have been followed for diagnosing the sickness and declaring a unit as sick (1.11.2);

2.10.6 the viability studies conducted for some of the sick units were not based on any systematic approach (1.11.3);

2.10.7 the rehabilitation measures had been recommended for only a few sick units and even those too were not comprehensive at all (1.11.3); and

2.10.8 the cases of the units sick since inception revealed that lop-sided emphasis on some aspects or neglect of one or more key aspects in the planning and management, were the main reasons for the sickness of these units (1.11.4).

2.11 Analysis of the cases of turning points of select sample units revealed that

2.11.1 quality of entrepreneurship was the key-factor in determining the course of sample SSI units (1.12.1);

2.11.2 though the select units belonging to the very successful group had faced many problems, the entrepreneurs could change the course of these units leading to outstanding performance by changing their business strategies (1.12.2);

2.11.3 almost the same (as above) was true in the case of select sample units belonging to the successful group (1.12.2);

2.11.4 the select sample units belonging to the average group had made only limited progress despite a good beginning because of the over dependence on market situations and lack of required entrepreneurial initiatives (1.12.2); and

2.11.5 the select units belonging to the sick group were languishing, despite good performance earlier in some cases, due to the inability of entrepreneurs to change the course of their enterprise by taking right kind of initiatives (1.12.2).

2.12 Analysis of regional variation in industrial characteristics and performance of sample units revealed that

2.12.1 sample SSI units in Bangalore district were larger and more capital intensive than those in the three backward districts of Gulbarga, Dharwar and Mysore (1.13.1 and 1.13.2).

2.12.2 sample SSI units in the three backward districts were more efficient in the utilization of capital and man power in comparison to that of those in Bangalore district (1.13.3).

2.12.3 the proportions of very successful units and average units were larger in Bangalore district while those of successful units and sick units were larger in other three backward districts (1.13.4).

III. SUGGESTIONS

3.1. While appraising the project-report of a small scale entrepreneur for financial assistance, the financing agencies should make sure whether the commercial viability of the proposed product has been well established. In case the commercial viability of the proposed product is yet to be established, financial support (term loan as well as working capital) entrepreneur should be provided under a special scheme on soft term basis for the first few years.

3.2. When the financial support for fixed investment for setting up a new SSI unit is provided by a term lending institution (e.g.,

KSFC), it should check as to whether the proposed unit would have sufficient working capital funds (including the working capital support from a bank).

3.3. A term lending institution, like KSFC, should have provision to provide working capital support in the form of short-term loans (may be on an annual basis) on a concessional rate of interest to such new SSI units as might have been assisted by it for investment in fixed assets but would not have been able to get adequate working capital support from a bank. Such assistance should be provided to a unit during its initial stage of operation (say for the first three years).

3.4. There should be a provision for extending working capital support in the form of short-term loan by a term-lending institution, like KSFC, also, to a viable sick SSI unit that may have been given financial support for fixed investment by KSFC but is not able to get working capital support from a bank. Such assistance would be useful in reducing the idling and wastage of fixed assets acquired by an entrepreneur with the financial support from the KSFC.

3.5. In the case of a SSI unit being set up as a partnership concern, an institution, like KSFC should seek undertakings from the partners that they would not desert the unit at least for the first three years since the commencement of production. This should apply particularly in the case of units in which the concerned partners are required to make significant contributions to the financial strength and production and marketing aspects of the unit.

3.6. An entrepreneur, who is setting up his SSI unit for the first time, should not go in for a large investment in the beginning itself. Instead, he should plan for the gradual growth of his unit. Small size of investment in the beginning would facilitate greater flexibility for the desired change and diversification of product-range in future. It may be noted that the units belonging to the very successful group had the smallest averge investment on fixed assets in the initial year. In fact, none of the units belonging to this group had more than Rs. 500,000 investment on fixed assets in the initial year.

3.7. An entrepreneur who wants to change his product or diversify his product-range, after running his unit for a few years, should be encouraged with liberal financial support from KSFC and banks.

3.8. It would be desirable for the financial institutions and banks to insist that an entrepreneur should undergo a short-term (4 to 6 weeks) training for small business management before setting up of his unit. Such training courses may be organised by management institutions, entrepreneurship development institutions, small industry service institutes, technical consultancy organisations, and district industries centres, etc. The financial support for such training courses should come from the national level and state level financial institutions, banks and fees to be charged from the entrepreneurs.

3.9. It was found that technical qualification, formal training, and previous work experience of entrepreneurs were not significantly associated with the performance-levels of sample SSI units. This may be so because a person generally receives education and training, and has experience in a particular discipline/area. Such qualifications, training and experience may not be adequate enough for an entrepreneur whose responsibility demands a multi-disciplinary and multi-area approach. Therefore, there is a need for developing comprehensive training packages based on real world situations for imparting entrepreneurial and managerial skills.

3.10. The procedures for securing financial assistance and infrastructural facilities, and getting approvals and sanctions should be rationalised and simplified so as to reduce the time-lag and unnecessary harassment to the prospective entrepreneurs. All the procedures after their rationalisation and simplification, should be grouped into two sets — one set for which approval and sanctions, etc. could be obtained simultaneously from the different offices, and the other set for which approval and sanction have to be secured in a sequential manner.

3.11. There is a need to pay greater attention for reducing delay with regard to the allotment of industrial shed, power-connection and telephone connection. For this, the State Small Scale Industrial Development Corporation (SSIDC) should have agreement or understanding with the concerned State Electricity Board and Telephone Department so that the power and telephone connections could be provided in an industrial shed within a limited period (not exceeding three months) after its allotment to an entrepreneur.

3.12. The State Electricity Board should ensure that power-cut, if any, to the SSI units in an industrial estate and in an industrial area is scheduled and notified. The power-cut to SSI units should be scheduled in such a way that it does not affect the production-schedule of SSI units — particularly those working on a single shift basis.

3.13. Government of India should enact laws stipulating a specific period for payment by the customers to SSI units for the goods supplied so that an entrepreneur could take the help of legal provision in case there is an inordinate delay in the realisation of bills. Since litigation in a general court of law is bound to be a time-consuming process, the government should set up tribunals for handling such cases. Also, there should be provision for additional working capital support from banks to the entrepreneurs, in dire need, during the litigation period and till the realisation of bills.

3.14. The institutes for training industrial workers should conduct potential surveys on an annual basis for assessing the requirement of industrial workers in different skills. Based on such surveys, each industrial training institute should plan its training programmes one year in advance and publicise the same through the mass media, like newspapers, radio and television to attract potential trainee-workers.

3.15. Management institutes, entrepreneurship development institutes, Small Industries Service Institutes, and Technical Consultancy Organisations should develop teaching materials and cases especially for training existing as well as potential small scale entrepreneurs, particularly in the areas of production management, financial management, labour management and marketing management. The focus of such management training courses should be on imparting skills for planning and problem-solving rather than merely as giving a conceptual understanding. The management training programmes may be scheduled in such a way as would enable a greater number of SSI entrepreneurs to undergo training programmes without affecting the day-to-day management of their units.

3.16. The procedure and required documentation under the provisions of excise duty should be simplified so that the entrepreneurs are not scared of coming into the net of excise duty. It may be desirable to fix the minimum amount of excise duty on different size-classes of turnover so as to reduce documentation load.

3.17. The procedure and documentation required for the sales tax also should be simplified and efforts should be made to reduce inter-state disparity, if not at the national level at least at the regional level, in the rates of sales tax. This may facilitate greater expansion of market and competition which may ultimately lead to the production of quality goods.

3.18. Government policies, rules and procedures should be made more attractive for the graduation of a unit from the small scale to the medium scale. This may require decentralisation and devolution of power.

3.19. The Industrial Area Development Boards should come forward to provide developed industrial plots to such entrepreneurs who want to shift from an industrial estate on account of the growth of their units requiring larger industrial accommodation. Some of the sample entrepreneurs were not in favour of their units growing to the level of medium scale because of the constraint of industrial accommodation.

3.20. The concerned official of financial institutions, banks, promotional agencies, and government departments should be trained in the areas of financial and promotional support to SSI units. Also, the concerned officials should be exposed to the problems of SSI units through field visits and interaction with the SSI entrepreneurs periodically. Such training and exposures would give a better understanding of SSI units to the concerned officials who would then be in a better position to appreciate the problems of SSI entrepreneurs.

3.21. If a SSI unit has acquired the symptoms of sickness and the same is reported by the concerned entrepreneur or noticed by the concerned official of financing bank and/or an institution, the concerned bank or financial institution should conduct a diagnostic study to detect causes of symptoms without any loss of time.

3.22. Depending on the findings of diagnostic study, the financing bank and/or institution should help the entrepreneur in initiating measures for preventing the sickness of his unit without loss of time.

3.23. If the diagnostic study reveals that a SSI unit has already become sick, the unit should be declared sick and a viability study of the unit should be conducted without further loss of time.

3.24. On the basis of the outcome of viability study, a decision for or against the rehabilitation of unit should be taken without any loss of time. Once a sick unit has been found viable and decision for its rehabilitation has been taken, a comprehensive rehabilitation package should be implemented for the revival of unit instead of resorting to some adhoc measures. Reserve Bank of India and IDBI have already issued comprehensive guidelines in this regard.

3.25. Utmost efforts should be made to reduce the time-lag in the whole process, starting from the symptoms of sickness being noticed to the implementation of rehabilitation measures. Time is a very important factor in business and it must be appreciated and honoured by the concerned officials of banks, financial institutions, promotional agencies and government departments.

3.26. In the success of a small business, more than the product and the project, what matters is the competence of the entrepreneur himself. Therefore, at the project appraisal stage it is necessary that the person as an entrepreneur also comes in for some scrutiny. This may be done by a group from the financing institution including a management professional from outside.

3.27. KSFC should devise a screening process so as to ensure that only a right person with right project is provided financial support. It may be noted that mere previous experience in a relevant field or technical competence of an entrepreneur or assurance for the purchase of his products in bulk by a few customers would not be sufficient enough to ensure the success of his enterprise as is evident from the findings of this study. Also, mere a good project report is not going to ensure the success of an enterprise. Today, one can obtain a project report of any specifications from consultants and others in the market against payment. KSFC should, therefore, not rely too much on mere soundness of a project report while deciding to provide financial support to an entrepreneur. The entrepreneurial qualities of the person behind a project are more important than his project and economic status.

3.28. The process of screening entrepreneurs by KSFC may comprise written tests as well as oral interaction. The focus of screening device should be on:

(A) personality traits of enterpreneur;

(B) depth of his knowledge regarding the proposed project; and

(C) adequacy of his skills and understandings required for the management of his enterprise.

(A) Personality Traits

(i) The strength of his achievement motivation and his power to influence others for getting the things done should be examined;

(ii) The second aspect of his personality trait to be examined should be his internal and external locus control. This would indicate as to whether he has control on his emotions and sentiments while taking business decisions or is likely to be carried away by emotions, expectations and excitment in his decision-making process. Also, whether he has clarity of thought and capacity to take cool and calculated business decisions even in the face of external and environmental pressures;

(iii) The third aspect to be examined would be his affiliation motive. This would indicate whether the person concerned has tendency to depend on others while taking vital business decisions or is confident of taking decision on his own. Also, whether he is capable of owning the resultant responsibility of his decisions in future or has tendency to blame others for the unfavourable results of his own decisions;

(iv) The fourth aspect to be examined should be an entrepreneur's sense of being honest to himself. This would indicate as to whether he would be prepared to accept the realities of situation obtaining in his own enterprise, in his surroundings and business environment, and would be flexible and sensitive enough to effect necessary changes in his business strategy as and when required or would be guided by carelessness and continue to waste his resources and energy on his eccentric ideas, expectations, and value system.

(B) Depth of his Knowledge Regarding Proposed Project

A screening committee should not be guided by mere the details of information furnished in an entrepreneur's project report but question him throughly on the different aspects of project proposed to be taken up by him. For this the following information may be sought from him.

(i) Whether entrepreneur knows the status of technology proposed to be used by him or not? Whether the proposed technology is a proven one or appropriate one or would require certain modifications? If it is not proven one or requires certain modifications, what is the nature and extent of risk involved in using such a technology and what safeguards including alternatives are available to him?

(ii) Whether the proto-type of proposed product is available and its commercial viability has been established? If not, is he aware of the time and resources required for the development of proto-type and establishing its commercial viability? What would happen if the new product fails to be commercially viable? What would be the nature and extent of risk involved, what would be the commercial implications of such a failure and also what alternatives would be available to him?

(iii) Has he done some sort of market survey and understood the costs of plant and machinery, supplier's and financing agency's terms and conditions, likely price escalation during the intervening period between placing of order and getting delivery? Has he made provision for financial contigencies arising in the wake of enhancement of price, custom duties, transportation charges and installation expenses, etc?

(iv) Has he estimated the nature and quantum of raw materials required, their availability in the domestic and foreign markets, major sources of supply, price stability or fluctuations in the recent past and likely in the near future?

(v) Has he estimated the size and type of accommodation required for his enterprise, its availability and terms and conditions? Also, whether he is aware of the types of facilities and services required to run his enterprise and their availability or likely availability in and around his enterprise and terms and conditions of these facilities and services?

(vi) Has he estimated the man power requirement and its availability? Would the required skilled personnel would be available or he would have to train them? If he has to train them, what would be its likely impact on the quality of his product and cost of production in the initial stages?

(vii) Does he know how to compute break-even point, has he estimated the likely fixed costs and variable costs? When is his unit expected to reach its break-even point and what would be the profit margin after the break-even stage? Would he be able to generate sufficient surplus to service his debt after the break-even stage and if so how long would it take for him to make full repayment of the loan borrowed for fixed investment?

(viii) Has he conducted market survey to identify market for his products and marketing channels for distribution? How is he going to decide about his pricing policy? Is he going to emphasis on quality products and if so what measures would he take to maintain and improve the quality of his products? What is his attitude towards service after sales?

(C) Management of Enterprise

The screening committee should test his skills of managing an enterprise, his awareness of likely managerial problems, the means and ways of overcoming the managerial problems. These may be examined with regard to:

(i) Production Management,

(ii) Financial management, accounting and importance of Balance Sheet,

(iii) Marketing management,

(iv) Labour management, Factory Act and Labour laws,

(v) Management of negotiations with Govt. departments, financial agencies, support agencies and customers and suppliers,

(vi) Awareness of taxation rates, duties, and regulatory

provisions, and so on.

Such a screening test should be essential for all the aspiring/applicant entrepreneurs who wish to invest above Rs. 200,000 on plant and machinery of their proposed units. In the case of other aspiring/applicant entrepreneurs, a simplified version of the same screening tests should be conducted. All the three sets (A, B & C) of tests should be evaluated separately in order to know whether an aspiring/applicant entrepreneur's performance is good or poor in all the three tests or in a specific test. The total marks for written tests could be 70, and oral test 30. The 70 marks allotted for the written test may further be broken into–

(i) 20 marks for personality traits,
(ii) 30 marks for the knowledge of proposed project, and
(iii) 20 marks for management skills.

If the performance of an aspiring/applicant entrepreneur is only upto 50 per cent or below, he should be asked to undergo motivation training or opportunity guidance and project counselling or management training or a complete entrepreneurship training as per his performance.

KSFC may organise such screening tests for a group of aspiring/applicant entrepreneurs at its Regional Offices and Head Office depending on the convenience of KSFC as well as aspiring/applicant entrepreneurs. Training programmes may be organised by KSFC in collaboration with other concerned organisations, like SISI, DICs, TECSOK, banks and entrepreneurship and management training institutions. Further, such training programmes should not be completely free of costs and a reasonable fee should be charged from the trainees.

If an applicant entrepreneur is not willing to undergo such a training despite his poor performance in the screening tests, his application should be rejected outright without having any second thought. If an aspiring entrepreneur, irrespective of the nature and length of his previous experience, is not willing to invest even a small amount of his time and resources in learining the nuts and bolts of his business, he is unlikely to remain committed to his business and succeed in his venture.

3.29. KSFC may promote a cadre of project counsellors and management consultants who would provide escort services to entrepreneurs on various aspects of–

(i) Project-report preparation and assist them in seeking the necessary facilities and support from the concerned agencies in the pre-investment stage;
(ii) Implementation of project; and
(iii) Management of enterprise in the post-investment stage.

Such personnel may be trained in the field of opportunity guidance, project counselling, project management, and enterprise management. At least one such officer should be posted at each of the Branch and Regional Offices of KSFC. These officers should be equipped with the necessary facilities and authority to deal with the entrepreneurs and concerned agencies and be accountable for the promotion of quality entrepreneurship in their functional areas (territories).

3.30 The present study was conceived as an exploratory study and its findings indicate that there is need for further studies having focus on specific aspects. In this context, the following may be looked into —

(i) Possibility of conducting a similar study with large samples (say 1000 units) in Karnataka and other states,
(ii) Possibility of conducting a similar study at the national level, the findings of which can be generalised for the nation as a whole,
(iii) Possibility of conducting studies to know impact of the promotion of SSI on regional development and regional variation in the performance of SSI units because of variation in the socio-economic characteristics of each region,
(iv) Possibility of conducting in-depth studies on individual industry groups as per the national classification of industries,
(v) Development of cases with focus on different aspects of management such as production management, financial management, marketing management, labour management, and so on,

(vi) Development of cases on entrepreneurial excellence and failures.

The present study can be a base study for undertaking the studies as suggested above.

BIBLIOGRAPHY

Akhouri, MMP (1978) : Planning and Monitoring Entrepreneurship, in *Developing Entrepreneurship : A Handbook*; Eds. T Venkateswara Rao, Udai Parik, et.al; IIM Ahmedabad, pp. 336-47.

Alexander, PC (1963) : *Industrial Estates in India*, Asia Publishing House.

Bandyopadhyay, Kalyani (1969) : Industrialization Through Industrial Estates, Bookland Pvt. Ltd.

Berna, James J (1960) : Industrial Entrepreneurship in Madras State, Asia Publishing House, Bombay.

Bhanushali, SG, (1987) : *Entrepreneurship Development : An Interdisciplinary Approach*, Himalaya Publishing House.

Bhatia, BS and RK Sharma (1989) : Entrepreneurship Performance in a Developing Economy : A Case Study of Punjab; in *Entrepreneurship Development in India*; Eds. Sami Uddin, Mittal Publications, Delhi, pp. 177-90.

Chattopadhyay, Somnath (1978) : Strategies of Motivation Development, in *Developing Entrepreneurship : A Handbook*; Eds. T. Venkateswara Rao, Udai Parik, et.al, Learning Systems, pp. 126-48.

Cohn, Theodore, Roy A Lindberg (1974) : *Survival and Growth : Management Strategies for the Small Firm*, AMACOM.

Das, NC (1989) : An Insight into the Entrepreneurship Development Programme of the North-East India, in *Entrepreneurship Development in India*, Eds. Sami Uddin; Mittal Publications, Delhi, pp. 237-42.

Development Commissioner, SSI Ministry of Industry, G.O.I. (1985) : *Diagnostic Survey Regarding Sickness in the Small Scale Units*; GOI, New Delhi.

Deeks, John (1976) : *The Small Firm Owner—Manager: Entrepreneurial Behaviour and Management Practices*, Praeger Publishers.

Deshpande, MU (1982) : *Entrepreneurship of Small Scale Industries*, Deep and Deep Publications, New Delhi.

Deshpande, MV Panvalkar (1980) : Developing Entrepreneurship — Need for a Planned and Coordinated Effort, in *Entrepreneurship Development Programmes*, IDBI, Bombay, pp. 39-58.

Desai, Vasant (1983) : *Problems and Prospects of Small-Scale Industries in India*, Himalaya Publishing House, Bombay.

Entrepreneurship Development Institute of India (EDII) (1987) : Developing New Entrepreneurs, EDII Ahmedabad.

Frantz, Forrest H (1978) : Successful Small Business Management, Prentice-Hall, INC, Englewood Cliffs, New Jersy.

Gaikwad, VR and RN Tripathy (1970) : *Socio-psychological Factors Influencing Industrial Entrepreneurship in Rural Areas : A Case Study in Tanku Region of West Godavari, A.P*, National Institute of Community Development, Hyderabad.

Goldar, Bishwanath (1988) : Relative Efficiency of Modern Small Scale Industries in India, in *Small Scale Industries in Industrial Development: The Indian Experience*, Eds. KB Suri, Sage Publications India Pvt. Ltd., New Delhi, pp. 95-117.

Goswami, Dileep (1987) : *Practical Handbook for Revival of Sick Industries*, EMCON Business Review, New Delhi.

Hukku, VN (1988) : *Management in Young Enterprises*, Radha Publications, New Delhi.

IDBI (1980) : *Study of IDBI Assisted Industrial Estates*, Mimeo, IDBI, Bombay.

Jalan, Bimal (1978) : Production in Tiny, Small and Large Scale Sectors — A Note, *Economic and Political Weekly*, May 20, pp. 852-54.

Kashyap, SP (1988) : Growth of Small-size Enterprises in India : Its Nature and Content, *World Development*, Vol.16, No.6, pp. 667-81.

Khandelwal, NM (1985) : *Working Capital Management in Small Scale Industries*, Ashish Publishing House, New Delhi.

Little, Ian MD, Dipak Mazumdar and John M Page, Jr. (1987) : *Small Manufacturing Enterprises : A Comparative Study of India and Other Economies*, Oxford University Press, p. 202.

Macfarlane, William N (1977) : *Principles of Small Business Management*, McGrow Hill Book Company.

Marting, Elizabeth, Eds. (1970) : *Management for the Smaller Company*, DB Taraporevala Sons & Co., Bombay.

Mazumdar, HK and A Nag (1977) : *Survey of Mortality of Small Scale Industries in South India*, Indian Institute of Economics, Hyderabad.

Mohanty, Bedabati (1986) : *Economics of Small Scale Industries*, Ashish Publishing House, New Delhi.

Nagaiya, D (1971) : *Industrial Estate Programme : The Indian Experience*, SIETI, Hyderabad.

Patel, VG, Anil Srivastava (1978) : Small Enterprise Performance : Relevance of Managerial Competence, *ASCI Journal of Management*, Vol.7, No.2, March 1978, pp. 136-50.

Patel, VG (1981) : *Innovations in Banking : The Gujarat Experiments*, IDBI, Bombay.

Patel, VG (1987) : Entrepreneurship Development Programmes in India, in *Developing New Entrepreneurs*, EDII, Ahmedabad, pp. 1-40.

Pathak, HN (1975) : *Problems of Small Scale Entrepreneurs : Report on Study based in Gujarat*, IDBI, Bombay.

Pattanaik, SM (1988) : *Development Strategy for Small Industries*, Himalaya Publishing House, Bombay.

Philip, J, Vinod, K Tewari and AN Pandey (1988) : *Small Scale Industries — Growth and Sickness*, Unpublished, IIM, Bangalore.

Planning Commission (1980) : *Sixth Five Year Plan*, GOI, New Delhi.

Planning Commission (1985) : *Seventh Five Year Plan*, GOI, New Delhi.

Pradhan, Gopinath (1985) : *Industrial Estate and State Development*, Criterion Publication, New Delhi.

Ramaiah, et.al (1987) : Sickness in Units Financed by APFC, *SEDME*, Vol. Nov.-June, 1987, pp. 31-38.

Ramakrishnan, P (1988) : *New Entrepreneurship in Small Scale Industry in Delhi*.

Raghunathan, N (1988) : Role and Performance of Small Scale Industries in the National Economy, Paper presented at the Seminar on *Small Scale Indsutries and the National Economy*, held at Bangalore, Nov. 27-29.

Rao, T Venkateswara, Prayag Mehta (1978) : Psychological Factors in Entrepreneurship, in *Developing Entrepreneurship — A Handbook*, Eds. TV Rao et.al., Learning Systems.

Rao, N Gangadhara (1986) : *Entrepreneurship and Growth of Enterprise in Industrial Estates*, Deep & Deep Publications, New Delhi.

Reddy, KC (Ed.) (1988) : *Sickness in Small Scale Industries*, Ashish Publishing House, New Delhi.

Reserve Bank of India (RBI) (1976) : *Sick Industrial Undertakings*, DBOD No. CAS.BC 133/C.466 (514) -76, Bombay, November 26.

Reserve Bank of India (RBI) (1978) : *Sick Industries-Small Scale Units*, DBOD.No.CAS.BC.64/C 4469 SIUO-78, Bombay, May 12.

Reserve Bank of India (RBI) (1987) : *Rehabilitation of Sick Small Scale Industrial Units*, RDCD No. PL.NFS.BC 48/ SIU-20-87, Bombay, February 6.

Saxena, KK (1987) : *Regional Input-Output Model for Small Scale Industries*, Himanshu Publications.

Scarborough, Norman M, Thomas W Zimmerer (1988) : *Effective Small Business Management*, Merril Publishing Company, Columbus, Ohio.

Sharma, KL (1975) : *Entrepreneurial Performance in Role Perspective*, Abhinav Publications, New Delhi

Sharma, KL, Harnek Singh (1980) : *Entrepreneurial Growth and Development Programmes in North India : A Sociological Analysis*, Abhinav Publications, New Delhi.

Shetty, Majur C, Somnath, Nagendra P Singh (1980) : Development of Entrepreneurship—Some Highlights of Experiences of Development Banking Centre in, *Entrepreneurship Development Programmes*, IDBI, Bombay, pp. 64-76.

Shirodkar, DM (1988) : Financial Support to Small Scale Industries by IDBI, Paper presented at the *Seminar on Promoption and Management of Small Scale Industries — Issues and Problems*, held at Bangalore, Feb.18-20.

Shivaramu, S (1985) : *Entrepreneurship and Enterprise Growth*, Seema Publications, New Delhi.

SIETI (1974) : *Socio-psychological Factors Influencing the Adaptation of the Innovation of Starting A Small Industrial Unit*, SIETI, Hyderabad.

Siropolis, Nicholas C. (1977) : *Small Business Management : A Guide to Entrepreneurship*, Houghton Miffin Company, Boston.

Shivaraman, Usha & Navika Chander (1989) : Is Small Sick?, *The Economic Times, Midweek Review*, Bangalore, May 18, p. iii.

Sonal (1989) : Region-wise Industry-wise Analysis, *The Economic Times, Mid-Week Review*, Bangalore, May 18, p. ii.

Srinivasan, G (1989) : Young Entrepreneurship in Pondicherry Area, in *Entrepreneurship Development in India,* Eds. Sami Uddin, Mittal Publications, Delhi

Srivastava, SB (1981) : *A Practical Guide to Industrial Entrepreneur,* Sultan Chand & Sons, New Delhi

SBI (1975) : *Role of Bank in Effective Growth of Small Scale Industries, Report of the Study Team of the State Bank of India,* Bombay

SBI Rehabilitation Cell Regional Office Visakhapatnam (1988) : Weakness of SSI, in *Sickness in Small Scale Industries,* Eds. KC Reddy, Ashish Publishing House, New Delhi.

Steinhoff, Dan (1978) : *Small Business Management Fundamentals,* McGraw-Hill Book Company, p. 298

Subrahmanian, KK, Kashyap, SP (1975) : Small-Scale Industry — A Trend Report, in *A Survey of Research in Economics,* ICSSR pp. 76-112

Taub, Richard P and Doris L Taub (1989) : *Entrepreneurship in India's Small-Scale Industries : An Exploration of Social Contexts,* Manohar Publications.

Tewari Vinod K, Amar Nath Pandey (1986) : *Small Industries Under District Credit Plan in India,* Mimeo, IIM Bangalore.

INDEX